Web Offset Press Troubles

compiled by

Robert F. Reed

THIRD EDITION

revised by

David B. Crouse

Graphic Arts Technical Foundation
4615 Forbes Avenue
Pittsburgh, Pennsylvania 15213

Library of Congress Catalog Card Number: 77-094463
International Standard Book Number: 0-88362-023-5

This publication was originally made available
through the assistance of a Special Merit Grant
from the Office of State Technical Services,
Division of the United States Department of
Commerce, Washington, D.C.

Contents

9. Ink Troubles

Foreword

This book was originally compiled as the result of an extensive survey conducted throughout the web offset industry. As part of the survey, experienced people, representing both suppliers and printers, were asked their opinions concerning the causes and controls of problems that were troubling web offset printers. Conflicts in opinion were resolved where possible, and the results were assembled into usable form and became the first edition of this book. It was true at that time and is still true that many of the suspected causes and remedies have not been verified through scientific investigation. Each statement, however, is supported by persons highly knowledgeable in the field of web offset printing.

The third edition of this book contains significant changes, both additions and deletions, from the second edition. These changes have been incorporated mainly as a result of the extensive research work in the field of web offset printing by GATF. In addition, the book *Web Offset Press Operating* was published in January 1974. The two books are meant to complement each other, the operating book as a general instructional text and this book as a ready reference for specific problems.

Web offset is an extremely complex operation, and there is a great deal about its operation that is not yet known. For this reason, GATF welcomes your comments and additions regarding the information contained here. Such additional information will be collected for inclusion in future editions. Your cooperation will help to provide a better book for future users.

David B. Crouse
Supervisor, Engineering Division
Research Department

January 1979

Preface

Web presses have been used extensively in most mechanical printing processes, particularly in newspaper and magazine printing by letterpress and rotogravure, as well as in flexography. The wide use of web presses in offset printing is more recent and has grown tremendously during the past twenty years. Its growth has been due principally to the adaption to lithography of heatset ink techniques.

Although the web offset method has become an important factor in lithographic production, the web method still involves many problems, some of which are due to press construction. Press and auxiliary equipment manufacturers are still experimenting, and changes are constantly being made. Paper, ink, and blankets for web offset are continually undergoing refinement.

While the basic printing in web offset is the same as in sheetfed offset, the mechanics of handling paper and of drying the printed web are different. The auxiliary equipment required to perform various finishing operations on web presses has no place on sheetfed presses, where these operations are carried out in the bindery or other finishing areas.

Know-how and experience in sheetfed offset press operation are a help to a web offset pressman but are far from enough to equip him to run a web offset press. Because of the many mechanical differences, considerable instruction and months of practice are needed before he gains reasonable efficiency. For this reason, and because of the rapid growth of web offset, there is a shortage of experienced operators.

Web Offset Press Troubles has been published by GATF to help web offset pressmen and their crews gain knowledge and efficiency. The book defines the many troubles commonly encountered in day-to-day press operation and offers the best remedies known at present. These are not one man's opinions but have been contributed by many recognized authorities in the industry. It is realized that some of the remedies suggested cannot ordinarily be carried out by an operating crew without authority from supervision and/or management who know best the demands of schedules and quality. And in some cases, the suggested remedies require special equipment not on hand.

GATF hopes that *Web Offset Press Troubles* will be of help in advancing knowledge and in improving quality and efficiency in web offset production. The aim has been to use all terms in their commonly accepted sense. This policy has been adopted to avoid adding to some of the confusion that already exists in the interpretation of many widely used web offset terms.

GATF gratefully acknowledges the cooperation of the following persons for their criticisms and helpful suggestions during the preparation or revision of this book:

Harvey A. Buntrock
William H. Bureau
Joseph P. Casey
John P. Corcoran
Joseph G. Curado
Thomas Fadner
Karl Fox
Werner Gerlach
Jack V. Greco
Paul J. Hartsuch

Roy Hensel
C. Houtkamp
A. Keesen
William W. Lester
A. P. Peterson
Ray Prince
Thomas Taylor
Ken L. Wallace
John C. Wurst

1 Introduction

History

Web offset presses are a comparatively recent development. Prior to World War II, almost all lithographic presses were sheetfed, and the trend was toward larger multicolor presses. While a few web offset presses were in operation, these were used mostly for single-color and simple two-color work where high quality was not required. These web offset presses had no heat dryers through which to pass the freshly printed web.

While heatset letterpress printing had started in the 1930s, heatset offset inks had not yet been developed. However, the success of heatset letterpress printing made the heatset principle a prime objective in web offset. As a result, heatset offset inks were developed, and heat dryers began to be installed in 1948. Since then, improvements in presses, printing plates, blankets, dryers, paper, and ink have contributed greatly to the success and growth of web offset printing.

The adoption of web offset was slow at first but has accelerated amazingly since about 1950. Manufacturers are now building web offset presses for publication, commercial color, newspaper, business form, and job work. There are also some combination presses. In recent years the greatest growth increase has been in the field of four- to six-color blanket-to-blanket heatset presses.

A five-color blanket-to-blanket web offset press. *Courtesy of Graphic Systems Division/Rockwell International*

During this growth period, there has been some trend toward "standard" size groups. The predominant group has been in the web widths of 36 to 38 in. (0.91 to 0.97 m) with cutoff (fixed) in the range of 22 1/2 to 23 9/16 in. (0.57 to 0.60 m). Very recently a new "standard" group has begun to develop around the web width of 19 to 26 in. (0.48 to 0.66 m). Presses with web widths of more than 80 in. (2 m) have been placed in production.

The multicolor web offset presses being built require heatset inks and are being used to print magazines, trade journals, catalogs, encyclopedias, books, general publicity, brochures, and the finest commercial color work.

A small blanket-to-blanket web offset newspaper press. Note the absence of dryer and chill sections.
Courtesy of the Goss Company

Local newspapers are rapidly converting to web offset, and most multiple business form work is done by web offset. But the equipment used consists of specialty presses, which are not covered in this book.

Obviously, the popularity and growth of web offset have been phenomenal. Some of the growth has been due to business that was formerly printed by letterpress or gravure. In many cases, web offset actually has created new printing business because of the economies it offered to the printing buyer.

Types of web offset presses

The printing method on a lithographic web offset press is essentially the same as on a sheetfed lithographic offset press. There are plate and blanket cylinders, and dampening and inking systems. The only difference is that plate and blanket cylinders have practically no gaps. However, the method of obtaining the impression varies with press design, of which there are three general types: blanket-to-blanket, common-impression-cylinder, and in-line.

Typical blanket-to-blanket printing unit.

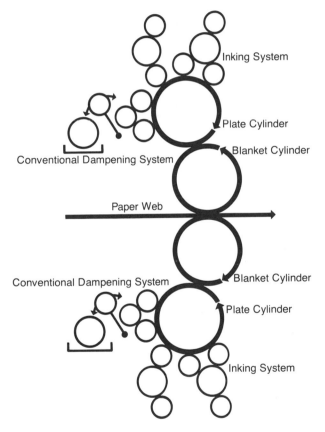

Inking System

Plate Cylinder

Blanket Cylinder

Conventional Dampening System

Paper Web

Conventional Dampening System

Blanket Cylinder

Plate Cylinder

Inking System

By far the most popular type of commercial web offset press prints blanket-to-blanket. The paper web passes between two blanket cylinders, each of which acts as the impression cylinder for the other. Primarily a perfecting press, a blanket-to-blanket press prints on both sides of the web in one pass. The number of colors printed is dependent on the number of printing units. The actual number of units depends on the need to print special colors (over and above the "normal" four colors), to varnish, to print double-text runs, or to use multiple webbing.

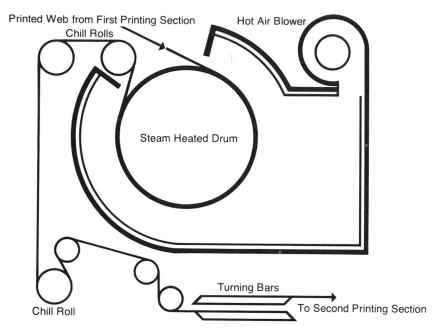

Drum dryer used on a common-impression-cylinder web offset press.

Another type of web offset press is the common-impression-cylinder press. A large, steel impression cylinder is common to all the units which print on one side of the web. To perfect, there are usually two presses in tandem. The web is printed on one side in the first press, dried, turned, backed up in the second press, dried, and delivered, all in one

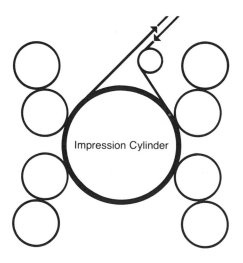

The common-impression-cylinder press, often called a drum press.

operation. On a double-ender press, a half-width web is printed and dried, then fed back, turned, and backed up on the other side of the same press, all in one operation.

A third type of press is the in-line press (see figure). Each unit consists of a plate cylinder (with the required inking and dampening systems), a blanket cylinder, and a steel impression cylinder.

The in-line press, used for forms, cartons, and other kinds of one-sided printing.

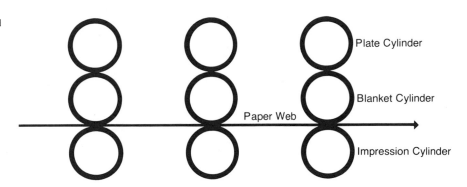

Plate Cylinder

Blanket Cylinder

Paper Web

Impression Cylinder

Specialized and auxiliary equipment

There are more in-line presses than any other type of web offset press, and they are used for forms, labels, boxboard, wrappers, and all other types of single-sided printing done by web offset. To perfect, a turning bay is added to the press.

Specialized equipment needed to handle the web makes the web offset press differ from the sheetfed offset press in the following ways:

1. The infeed is from rolls.

2. Register depends on web tension and web side lay controls.

3. For most work, heat dryers integral with the press are required.

Roll stand and infeed on a web offset press. *Courtesy of the Miehle Company*

One form of tunnel dryer used on common-impression-cylinder web offset presses.

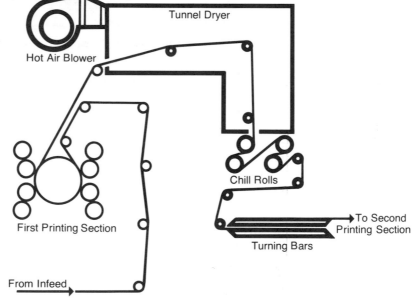

4. Chill rolls are used to set the ink, which is semifluid as the web comes from the dryer. Some presses are equipped with remoisturizing sprays or roller coaters, which replace some of the water removed from the paper during the pass through the dryer and combat static on "sheet" delivery.

Heat dryer and chill rolls, with one type of remoisturizing unit.

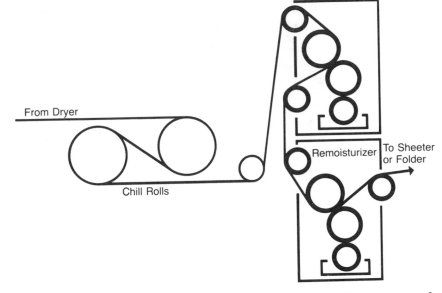

From Dryer

Chill Rolls

Remoisturizer

To Sheeter or Folder

5. Depending on the nature of the printed product, one of two general types of delivery is used. These types are (1) sheet delivery and (2) folded signature delivery.

Sheet delivery on blanket-to-blanket web offset press.

Dryer exit, chill rolls, folder, and folded signature delivery on blanket-to-blanket web offset press. *Courtesy of Graphic Systems Division/Rockwell International*

6. With auxiliary equipment, the operations of imprinting, numbering, punching, perforating, interleaving, and gluing can also be performed as parts of the press operation.

Some of the differences between webfed and sheetfed offset simplify or facilitate printing; others complicate printing or create problems. The advantages predominate; otherwise, web offset would not be showing such remarkable growth.

Advantages   Some of these advantages are as follows:

1. Higher speeds than sheetfed. If we compare a 52x76-in. (1.32x1.93-m) sheetfed, four-color press with a 25x38-in. (0.64x0.96-m) blanket-to-blanket press, the web offset press will produce three to four times as many completely printed sheets (both sides) as the sheetfed press, with less total makeready time. This does not include the possible gains in finishing, such as in folding. Some presses, especially the common-impression-cylinder type, can produce as much as eight times the number cf printed sheets as the sheetfed press.

2. Blanket-to-blanket presses can print all colors on both sides of the web in one operation using a single dryer.

3. Adequate drying of heatset inks usually takes place in a fraction of a second. Antisetoff sprays are not needed.

The multiwebbed blanket-to-blanket press with four webs, each printed one color both sides.

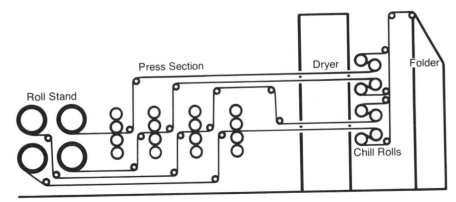

4. The press can deliver the printed work as sheets, or it can slit, fold, and deliver signatures. With auxiliary equipment, it can imprint, number, perforate, punch, interleave, and glue — operations normally performed in the bindery.

5. Lightweight papers that give trouble on sheetfed presses are handled easily. No sheet feeder, sheet guides, insertion devices, grippers, or transfer cylinders are required. Embossing and curl are reduced.

6. Some low-cost letterpress coated papers can be printed without serious picking or piling trouble. This printability can represent a considerable reduction of paper costs.

7. Heatset inks lie mostly on the paper surface, giving better color and higher gloss with less ink.

8. Plate and blanket cylinders have practically no gaps. A narrow gap enables more even dampening and inking of plates.

9. Paper in rolls is cheaper than the same paper in sheet form.

10. Blanket-to-blanket presses can be multiwebbed. A four-unit blanket-to-blanket press can thus print two colors on both sides of two webs, one color on both sides of four webs, or a combination of four colors, two colors, and

one color by webbing one printing couple as a direct lithographic unit. The limiting factor is the number of roll stands with which the press is equipped.

11. The same press will print different web widths up to the maximum.

Dis-advantages

Some disadvantages and limitations of web offset are as follows:

1. The cutoff is determined by the cylinder circumference, so one dimension of the form is fixed. Layouts must meet this requirement.

2. Makeready cannot be done with waste sheets as in sheetfed offset. New paper must be used, and this increases waste.

3. Running waste is high. Average running waste is usually between 5% and 15%.

4. Wrappers and nonreturnable cores increase white waste.

5. Because of the high speed of web presses, register is more difficult to control.

6. Because most web offset presses have relatively small cylinders, they lack some of the accessibility of sheetfed presses for cleaning and adjustments.

The foregoing is a brief, generalized discussion of webfed offset presses and their essential parts and uses. For additional information, refer to the following GATF publications:

What the Printer Should Know about Paper

What the Lithographer Should Know about Ink

Instruments and Controls for the Graphic Arts Industries

Web Offset Press Operating

2 Infeed Troubles

Introduction

The infeed stand of a web offset press is the structure which holds the roll or rolls of paper being fed into the printing units of the press. Auxiliary mechanisms vary, depending upon the type of paper being printed, the nature of the job, and the problems likely to be encountered.

Brake on Infeed Reel

The brake is used to match the amount of paper unwinding from the roll with the amount of paper being used by the press.

Dancer Roller

The dancer roller has two functions. The first is to set tension in the web, and the second is to control the brake on the infeed roll.

Principle of reel brake action controlled by position of the dancer roller.

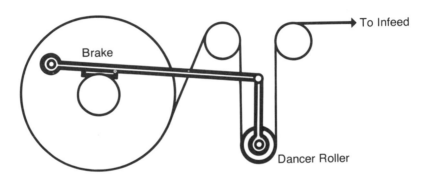

Tension in the infeed section of the press is a function of the effective weight of the dancer roller and is independent of its position. In examining the diagram, it can be seen that if the dancer roller weighs 200 pounds there will be 100 pounds of tension in the loop supporting the dancer roller regardless of whether the roller is high, low, or in the middle of its stroke.

The position of the dancer roller is used to control the brake on the infeed roll. If the dancer roller starts to rise, the press is using more paper from the dancer loop than is being supplied by the infeed roll. In such a case, the action of the brake is lessened, allowing more paper to flow from the infeed roll. If the dancer roller drops below its normal running position, the press is using less paper than is being supplied by the infeed roll. In this case, the action of the brake is increased, restricting the amount of paper being fed from the infeed roll.

Control of brake by rise and fall of the dancer roller, with tension constant.

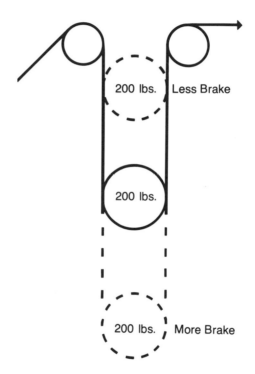

Metering Rollers

After it leaves the dancer roll, the paper web passes between metering rollers. These are rollers which have a positive grip on the web and usually are driven by a variable-speed drive. Tension going into the press is adjusted by changing the speed of the metering rollers. Metering rollers have little effect on dampening out tension variations that occur in the infeed section of the press.

Constant-Tension Infeed

Generally with today's equipment a constant-tension infeed requires the installation of a second dancer, or tension-sensing, roller. This second dancer is located between the infeed metering device and the press, and its signal is used to control the infeed metering device. This roller is not required to compensate for the amount of paper being used by the press and therefore is not used for storage. The stroke of this dancer is consequently quite small, reducing dancer-related tension variations. Because the infeed metering device offers inherently finer control than the roll stand brake, control by the second dancer is more precise. This second dancer can hold tension variations to a minimum, and so tension levels in the infeed can be higher without risking web breaks. This fact can lessen blanket wrap and elastic recovery in the printing units, providing better control of register.

Continuous-Web Infeed

There are two common methods that permit splicing the web from a new roll of paper to the running web without shutting down or slowing down the press to start the new roll. On both types, adhesive or two-sided adhesive tape is applied to the leading edge of the new roll.

In the first type, the flying splicer, the new roll is then brought up, as nearly as possible, to the same speed as the expiring web. At the proper moment, the running web is pressed against the pasted edge of the new roll, the stub end of the expiring web is automatically cut off, and the new roll begins to feed into the press.

One form of flying paster. *Courtesy of Graphic Systems Division/Rockwell International*

On the second type, the zero-speed splicer, a festoon is supplied that is capable of storing enough paper to run the press while the infeed is stopped to make the splice. When it is time to make a splice, the expiring roll is stopped and its web is pressed against the previously prepared leading edge of the new roll. The resulting splice is very similar to a mill splice in that it is quite strong and has a very short tail. After being spliced, the new roll is accelerated up to press speed, and the festoon is expanded, storing paper for the next splice.

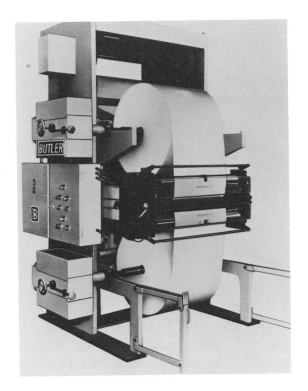

There are several advantages to this type of splicer. There is
no requirement for synchronizing the new and the old webs.
Rolls can be unwound in either direction, allowing the web
to be run either wire side or felt side up. A much wider
range of roll diameters can be spliced successfully because
there are no moving parts that have to be brought close to
the surface of the new roll.

Web Preheaters

The idea of preheating the web to increase its stability came
from gravure printing. In gravure, because of the necessity
of drying between units, there was a problem of keeping
the first printed image in register with subsequent images.
This problem developed because the web experiences its
greatest physical change the first time it goes through a
dryer. In order to minimize this effect, the web was run
through a dryer before the first printing unit — and
"preheaters" were born. Because the problems of web offset
printing are different from those of gravure, the preheater
has not been very successful. A lot of presses are equipped
with preheaters, but they are seldom used because of the

problem created by the hot metal in the preheater when the press is stopped. The one thing on which there seems to be general agreement is that the gas flame type of preheater does a reasonably good job of burning loose lint and fuzz off uncoated webs.

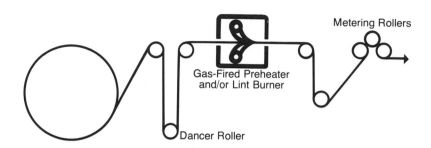

Web Preheater on the infeed of a web offset press.

Metering Rollers

Gas-Fired Preheater and/or Lint Burner

Dancer Roller

It should be kept in mind that if a preheater is being used to compensate for wet streaks in the web, the web temperature will have to be in the vicinity of 170°F (77°C) or higher. Such elevated temperatures in the web will create problems in the first printing units, and these can only be overcome by cooling the web down to more normal temperatures. This cooling requires the addition of chill rollers on the preheater. These rollers do not need to be press-driven but can be driven by the web.

Sheet Cleaner

The sheet cleaner is essentially a vacuum sweeper for removing loose paper dust and fibers that can cause imperfections in printing. It can cause a problem if the brush loosens material that is only partially bonded to the suface of the web.

This section on "Infeed Troubles" is intended to give the web offset pressman a ready reference that will help him (1) avoid infeed problems; (2) diagnose a problem quickly and correctly when it arises; (3) apply the proper remedy. Some of the remedies may not be possible under existing operating conditions — the press may not have the equipment or devices mentioned in a suggested remedy; it may not be possible to change the paper at the time;

doctoring heatset inks should be avoided. For a chronic infeed trouble that can only be overcome with equipment or devices not available on the press, the suggested remedy may serve as a guide to management in its investigations of new equipment. Where a remedy suggests changing paper or paper specifications, it is assumed that the paper supplier will be called in as soon as the trouble is identified as a paper problem; and correspondingly, the ink supplier when ink is concerned. For details on handling paper and paper complaints, see the "Paper Troubles" section.

Following are some troubles that originate in the infeed stand and its associated mechanisms:

Trouble: **Splice** does not hold.

Cause A: The web breaks at the splice before reaching the first printing unit.

Remedy 1:
On a flying paster, increase brush arm tension.

Remedy 2:
If two-sided tape is used, it may become covered with dust before the splice is made. Do not remove protective layer from tape until just before splice is to be made.

Remedy 3:
If glue is used, determine the longest time glue will still be "sticky" and not dry up or soak into the paper. If a prepared roll is held longer than 75% of this time, the roll should be reprepared.

Remedy 4:
With glue splicing, use a glue designed for the paper being run.

Remedy 5:
With paste or adhesive-tape splicing, make sure that the adhesive is properly applied.

Remedy 6:
With hand-splicing operations, check roll shaft and roll stand rollers for alignment.

Cause B: Too great a shock when a new roll is joined to the running web.

Remedy 1:
Make sure that the surface of the new roll is rotating at web speed before making the splice.

Remedy 2:
Check the timing of the splicing cycle, and correct if necessary.

Remedy 3:
When running lightweight papers, run with less infeed tension.

Trouble: **Web breaks** with no splice involved.

Cause A: Web tension is too great, or paper is too weak.

Remedy 1:
Adjust press elements that are not properly aligned. This problem can be identified by the appearance of wrinkles in a section of web. These wrinkles will run diagonally from corner to corner. Press elements in the area of the wrinkles should be trammed.

Remedy 2:
Adjust the linkage that actuates the reel brake to relieve the tension.

Remedy 3:
Reject weak paper.

Cause B: Foreign matter accumulating on the ends of the lead rollers, or loose grating on the ends of grater rollers.

Remedy:
Clean lead rollers, or repair grater rollers.

Cause C: Roll is out of round; this condition causes a sudden jerk with each revolution.

Storing rolls of paper on their sides, instead of their ends, can cause troublesome flats.

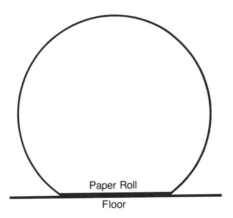

Paper Roll

Floor

Remedy 1:
Always store rolls of paper on their ends, especially when they are stack-stored.

Remedy 2:
Use care in handling rolls. Do not drop them or use excessive clamp pressure.

Cause D: Brake on infeed reel overheats. This can cause seizing and results in excessive tension. Generally, overheating occurs as the unwinding web approaches the core because of increasing reel speed.

Remedy:
Release brake control near end of roll and operate by hand.

Cause E: Ends of the roll are damaged. A crack or nick in the edge of the web becomes the starting point for a tear or break.

A paper roll with
damaged edge.
*Courtesy of
Kimberly-Clark Corp.*

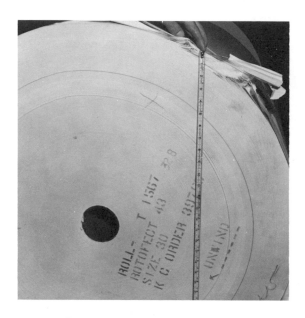

Remedy 1:
Prevention. Take care in handling rolls after removing
protective disks. A roll which is received in damaged
condition should be rejected or slabbed off to a point
below the damage, if the damage is near the outer layers.

Remedy 2:
Cut or sand any nicks out of end of roll. Take care to
leave no small cuts.

Cause F: Water in blanket gaps on start-up.

Remedy:
Reduce plate dampening to a minimum. If necessary, let
plate catch up at start; and clean up after press is up to
speed.

Cause G: Edge cracks, wrinkles, or slime holes are weak spots in the
web where tears or breaks can start.

Slime hole.
Courtesy of
Kimberly-Clark Corp.

Remedy:
None. These are defects in the paper, and if excessive, the stock should be set aside and the supplier notified.

Cause H: Uneven draw or tension on the paper web. This can be caused by a tapered roll, one with a nonuniform diameter.

Roll with nonuniform
diameter.

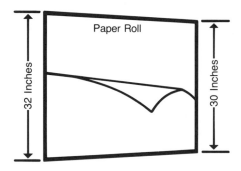

Remedy 1:
Adjust cocking roller.

Remedy 2:
Insist on receiving nontapered rolls.

Cause I: Speed of metering rollers is not synchronized with cylinder speed of the first printing unit.

Remedy:
Increase speed of the metering rollers. If metering drive is worn and will not give fine control, it should be repaired or replaced.

Trouble: **Web is not flat** as it feeds into the first printing unit.

Cause A: Web has nonuniform characteristics (basis weight, moisture content, etc.) from side to side.

Remedy 1:
Reweb the infeed section of the press to allow more time between unwinding and printing. Run with infeed tension as high as possible.

Remedy 2:
Adjust cocking roller to minimize problem.

Remedy 3:
Build up diameter of infeed roller under baggy area.

Cause B: Web is tight-edged because ends of roll were exposed to a dry atmosphere, and exposed edges shrank.

Remedy 1:
Best remedy is prevention. Specify moisture-proof wrapping. Reject rolls received with torn or damaged wrappings. (See Section 8, "Paper Troubles," for recommended roll handling procedures.)

Remedy 2:
Reweb the infeed section of the press to allow more time between unwinding and printing. Run with infeed tension as high as possible.

Cause C: Edges of the web are slack and floppy because of pickup of moisture from a humid atmosphere.

Remedy 1:
Best remedy is prevention. Specify moisture-proof wrapping. Reject rolls received with torn or damaged wrappings.

Remedy 2:
Reweb the infeed section of the press to allow more time between unwinding and printing. Run with infeed tension as high as possible.

Remedy 3:
Use tape or paper to build up that section of an infeed roller over which the slack edge of the paper rides.

Cause D: The web has lengthwise parallel ridges due to nonuniform moisture distribution, often called damp or wet streaks, or moisture welts.

Remedy 1:
Reweb the infeed section of the press to allow more time between unwinding and printing. Run with infeed tension as high as possible.

Remedy 2:
Spiral-wrap tape from center to outside of infeed roller so that web is stretched out laterally while running.

Spiral taping of roller to flatten out web.

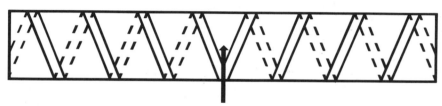

Direction of Web Travel

3 Printing Unit Troubles

Introduction   The printing unit on a blanket-to-blanket web offset press consists of two opposed (upper and lower) printing couples, each consisting of a blanket cylinder, a plate cylinder, a dampening system, and an inking system. The blanket cylinders act as impression cylinders for each other. Thus, a four-color blanket-to-blanket press has four printing units (four printing couples above and four below the web), and prints four colors on both sides of the web in one pass.

In common-impression-cylinder (C-I-C) presses, a large steel impression cylinder is common to two or more printing couples (satellites), each of which consists of one blanket cylinder and one plate cylinder with attendant dampening and inking systems. To perfect, the web is printed on one side and passed through a dryer, then turned, backed up, and dried again. The commonest method of achieving this result is to use two press sections with one dryer between them and another before delivery. In another design, there is only one press section and one dryer. A half-width web is printed on one side and passed through the dryer, then turned and backed up on the other side of the same press, passed through the dryer again, and delivered. A press of this latter design is generally called a "double-ender."

By far, most existing web offset presses are of the blanket-to-blanket types. These are more suitable for publications and general commercial color work than are common-impression-cylinder presses. The latter are designed primarily to meet special production requirements.

The plate and blanket cylinders on web offset presses differ from those on sheetfed presses by having very narrow gaps — as narrow as 0.375 inch (10 millimeters). Sheetfed presses need a wide gap in order to allow time to register and insert sheets. Web presses do not require this gap. Absence of a gap makes possible more uniform dampening and inking of the plates, since moisture and ink have no time to pile up on the form rollers between impressions.

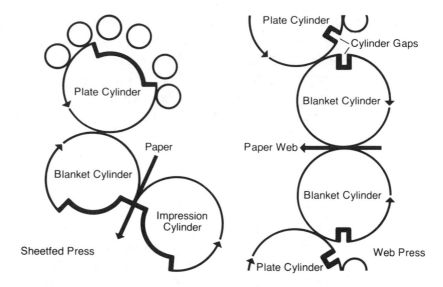

Cylinder gaps on sheetfed and web offset press cylinders.

On blanket-to-blanket presses, the plate and blanket cylinders are geared together and the two blanket cylinders are geared together. On common-impression-cylinder presses, the blanket cylinders are driven by a ring gear on the impression cylinder.

Proper functioning of the printing units depends on smooth driving and proper packing of the plates and blankets. Most plate and blanket cylinders have bearers to facilitate accurate alignment and provide the means for gauging the height or radius of plates and blankets. On most presses, the bearers run in contact under pressure as specified by the manufacturer. Bearer pressure tends to smooth out variations in power transmission caused by worn or faulty gears. On other presses, because bearers are spaced apart, cylinder alignment and spacing are adjusted by means of feeler gauges to attain proper clearance as specified by the manufacturer.

Plates and blankets are packed according to shop practices. Each press manufacturer specifies the proper conditions for his press. Usually, the recommended packing procedures call for plates to be 0.002-0.003 inches (0.05-0.075 millimeters) and blankets 0.000-0.001 inches (0.000-0.025 mm) over bearers. With the new compressible blankets, more squeeze is required, and plates and blankets must be packed higher. To maintain proper pressures, use of the packing gauge is important.

The press cylinders should be kept true and free from low spots. These could be caused by warpage, or by a rag, screw, washer, or other object going through the press. A bad paper wrap-up could bend the cylinder spindles and produce eccentricity. Damaged cylinders cannot function properly and should be repaired.

Most commercial presses are equipped with hollow ink vibrators for cooling the inking systems. This cooling is accomplished by pumping cold water through the vibrators. It should be remembered that such a system must also be able to pump warm water whenever the press is cold. Placement of the pump, modulating valve, and heater relative to the inkers for a typical system is shown in the diagram.

Typical press inker cooling system.

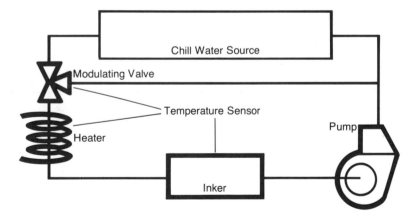

The temperature sensor controls both the modulating valve for cooling and the heater for heating. Common practice today is to locate the temperature sensor so that it controls either the temperature of the water going into the inker or the temperature of the water coming out of it. Because the cooling load varies with such things as ink tack, ink amount, press speed, etc., neither location is satisfactory. The accompanying table demonstrates this fact. Temperature variations in the inker caused by the changing heat load are shown in the right-hand column of the table. The values in the table are related by the accompanying formulas.

The table shows that rather severe changes in the average temperature occur if the sensor is located at either of the commonly accepted places designated T_1 or T_2. Only if the temperature of the water is sensed halfway through the system is it possible to maintain stable conditions. The equivalent of measuring at T_3 can be obtained by sensing at both T_1 and T_2 and averaging the results.

There are several advantages to be gained by having a constant-temperature system for the ink to work in. In the past these advantages have been to a large extent negated by the improper placement of the controlling sensor.

Effects on Inker Temperature Stability of Different Sensor Locations

Temperature Sensor Location	Heat Load (Btu/Min)	k	Temperature (°F)		
			W(I)	W(O)	Avg.
T_1	100	5	65	85	75
	200	5	65	105	85
	300	5	65	125	95
T_2	100	5	85	105	95
	200	5	65	105	85
	300	5	45	105	75
T_3	100	5	75	95	85
	200	5	65	105	85
	300	5	55	115	85

Web Offset Press Troubles   29

$$W_O = W_I + \frac{\text{Heat Load}}{k}$$

$$\text{Avg. Temp.} = \frac{W_I + W_O}{2}$$

W_I = Temp. of Water In (in °F)

W_O = Temp. of Water Out (in °F)

k = Proportionality Constant

T_1, T_2, T_3 : Locations of Temperature Sensor

Temperature sensing relationships.

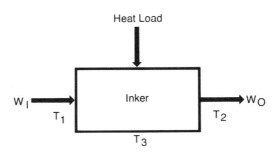

This section on "Printing Unit Troubles" is intended to give the web offset pressman a ready reference that will help him to: (1) avoid printing unit problems; (2) diagnose a problem quickly and correctly when it arises; (3) apply the proper remedy. Some of the remedies may not be possible under existing operating conditions — the press may not have the equipment or devices mentioned in the suggested remedy; it may not be possible to change the paper at the time; doctoring heatset inks should be avoided; a press mechanic may not be available in the plant, or he may not have the required equipment or parts on hand. For a chronic printing unit problem that can only be overcome with equipment or devices not available on the press, the suggested remedy may serve as a guide to management in its investigations of new equipment. Where the remedy suggests a major repair, this can serve as a signal to supervisory personnel that repair time must be scheduled. Where a remedy suggests changing paper or paper specifications, it is assumed that the paper supplier will be called in as soon as the trouble is identified as a paper problem; and correspondingly, the ink supplier when ink is concerned.

The principal troubles due to malfunctioning of web offset printing units and their causes and remedies are discussed here. Troubles connected with the inking and dampening systems are discussed in Sections 4 and 5. Paper and ink troubles are covered in Sections 8 and 9.

Trouble: **Gear streaks** in the printing are always parallel to the cylinder axis. Also, their pitch or distance apart is uniform and the same as the pitch of the teeth of the cylinder's driving gear.

Cause A: Improper packing of the plate and blanket. The blanket is trying to drive the plate cylinder, or vice versa, by surface contact. In other words, the surface drive is fighting the gear drive. The trouble usually occurs if there is not enough bearer pressure, if the gear teeth are worn, or if there is too much backlash.

Remedy:
To lessen the tendency of the driven cylinder to run ahead of the driving cylinder, the driven cylinder circumference should be made larger than that of the driving cylinder. On most presses, because the plate cylinder is gear-driven by the blanket cylinder, this difference is accomplished by removing packing from under the blanket and adding it under the plate.

Cause B: Lack of proper bearer pressure.

Remedy:
Check bearer pressure and if necessary reset according to manufacturer's specifications.

Cause C: Bottoming of gear teeth due to accumulation of fibers and dirt.

Remedy:
Clean the gear teeth and keep them clean and free from accumulated dirt and hardened lubricant by periodic cleaning.

Cause D: Worn cylinder bearings.

Remedy:
If remedies for A, B, and C do not help, replace the worn bearing.

Trouble: **Streaks** are parallel to the cylinder axis, but bear no relation to the pitch of the gear teeth.

Cause A: Worn cylinder bearings.

Remedy:
Replace worn bearings.

Cause B: Bouncing of inking or dampening rollers. One or more form rollers are set too hard against the plate. When they pass the cylinder gap, they strike the leading edge of the plate. This varies the ink films from end to end, producing a streak that is transferred to the plate after one revolution of the roller. Such streaks are worse if two or more rollers of the same size are set too hard against the plate. They are most objectionable on background color tints.

Remedy:
Reset the form rollers to proper pressure against the plate and drum. When setting form rollers, make certain that they are not being driven by the plate.

Cause C: Faulty bearings and too much pressure, or too little bearer pressure, between cylinders. These conditions will cause the two cylinders to move together when their gaps are in the nip between them. This movement of the cylinder will reduce the pressure between the cylinder and the cylinder or roller(s) that are in contact with the cylinder on the side opposite the gap.

Remedy 1:
Use the packing gauge to check the plate-to-blanket squeeze. If too high, remove the excess packing.

Remedy 2:
Check bearer pressure and increase if required.

Remedy 3:
Check cylinder bearings and replace if necessary.

Cause D: A loose and slipping blanket. A loose blanket may roll up and then slip on the blanket cylinder. This slippage is intermittent and causes streaks. The greater the plate-to-blanket pressure, the worse the slippage. (See also Section 4, "Ink Feed Troubles.")

Remedy 1:
Tighten the blanket.

Remedy 2:
Use the packing gauge to check the plate-to-blanket squeeze. If too much, remove the excess packing.

Trouble: **Uneven impression** can result from a number of conditions: uneven cylinder pressure, uneven or varying ink feed, stripped ink rollers, uneven dampening, poor or worn press plates, and defective blankets. Only uneven cylinder pressure will be discussed here; the other causes of uneven impression are discussed under "Ink Feed Troubles," "Dampening Troubles," and "Plate Troubles."

Cause A: Plate cylinder is warped or dented. To check this:

1. Remove the plate and packing.

2. Run the press with a thin film of ink on the form rollers, and lower the best form roller only until it contacts the highest parts of the cylinder surface. Take note of the depressed areas or spots.

Remedy 1:
Build up the depressed areas with tissue patches and shellac. Use fine sandpaper on a flat block to taper the edges and smooth down any high spots after the shellac has dried. This remedy in suggested only as a temporary measure.

Remedy 2:
For permanent correction, the cylinder should be built up by metal spraying, or by other means, and reground.

Cause B: The offset blanket is not uniform in thickness, or is embossed by swelling and/or curing of ultraviolet ink in image areas.

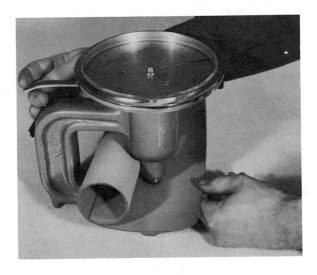

Use of the Cady gauge in measuring offset blanket thickness. Rolling blanket in throat of gauge enables measurements in all areas.

Remedy:
Replace the blanket.

Cause C: The blanket cylinder is dented or warped. To check this condition, first be sure that the plate cylinder is true and undented. (See Cause A.) Then follow this procedure: (1) Put on a plate and pack it exactly to bearer height. (3) Pack the blanket to 0.001 inch (0.025 millimeter) above bearers. (3) Ink up the dry plate and pull an impression on the blanket. Note the bare areas. (4) Turn the blanket end for end. Wash the blanket clean and pull another ink impression. If the bare areas remain in the same areas of the cylinder, after the blanket has been reversed, the blanket cylinder is dented or warped.

Remedy 1:
If the dent is not too deep, build it up with tissue torn to the required shape and applied with shellac. Use fine sandpaper on a flat block to taper the edges and smooth down any high spots after the shellac has dried. This procedure is recommended only as a temporary solution.

Remedy 2:
For permanent correction, the cylinder should be built up by metal spraying, or by other means, and reground.

Cause D: The impression cylinder is dented or warped. (This applies to common-impression-cylinder presses but not to blanket-to-blanket presses.) To check this condition first be sure that on at least one unit the plate and blanket cylinders are true and that the blanket is free from low spots. (See Causes A, B, and C.) Then roll up the blanket with a thin film of ink, and bring it up to the impression cylinder a little at a time until ink just begins to transfer. This procedure will show up any depressions in the impression cylinder.

Remedy:
A dented or warped impression cylinder should be built up by metal spraying, or by other means, and reground.

Cause E: Plate and blanket cylinders are not parallel, or blanket cylinders on a blanket-to-blanket press are not parallel. On a common-impression-cylinder press, blanket and impression cylinders may not be parallel. This condition will show up as a lack of impression on either or both sides when the tests outlined in C or D are made.

Remedy:
Follow instructions in the manufacturer's press operating manual, or call in a serviceman to parallel the cylinders.

Cause F: Dirty cylinder bearers. Dirt on a bearer lifts that end of the cylinder, causing less pressure.

Remedy:
Keep bearers clean at all times.

Trouble: **Slurring** is the filling-in of halftone shadows and the appearance of fringes at the back edges of solids. This trouble occurs mostly when printing on coated paper. Slurring is caused by slippage in the impression nip between the plate and blanket or between the blanket and the paper. On common-impression-cylinder presses, slurring can occur in either nip. But on blanket-to-blanket presses, it occurs mostly in the plate-to-blanket nip. Slurring (as opposed to doubling) can be identified by use of the GATF Star Target (see GATF Research Progress Report 52).

Enlargements showing slur in a halftone: (A) normal print; (B) unusually bad slur; (C) same areas as in A but with slur in shadow tone.

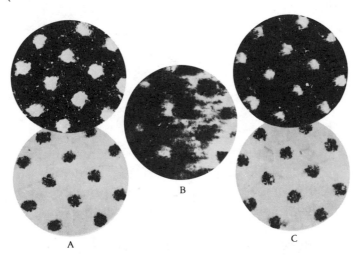

Cause A: Too much blanket-to-paper pressure on common-impression-cylinder presses.

Remedy:
Reduce the printing pressure to a minimum.

Cause B: Too much plate-to-blanket pressure, especially when running smooth, or ungrained, plates.

Remedy:
Reduce the plate-to-blanket pressure. Very smooth plates require no more than about 0.002 inch (0.05 millimeter) of impression.

Cause C: Running too much ink on coated stock. Excessive ink acts as a lubricant and aggravates slippage between plate and blanket.

Remedy:
Reduce ink feed. If this reduces color or black density, reduce the water feed. If necessary, use a little wetting agent in the fountain solution to reduce the amount required. Adding isopropyl alcohol to the fountain solution will accomplish the same result. The less the plate moisture, the less ink is required to give the desired coverage. If necessary, get a more highly pigmented ink and run less of it.

Cause D: Ink is too thin.

Remedy 1:
Use an ink with more body.

Remedy 2:
Reduce printing pressures to the minimum.

Cause E: Piling of paper coating on the printing areas of the blanket. Usually this starts in the middletone on the second or later unit of a multicolor press when printing coated stock. It produces a mottled pattern caused by slurred dots.

Remedy:
Switch to a more moisture-resistant coated stock. (See also "Paper Troubles: Paper Coating Piles.")

Trouble: **Doubling** is a register problem that can occur either between units or within a unit. Most doubling probably occurs between the plate and blanket within a printing unit. The problem can arise because all of the ink on the blanket is not transferred to the paper during each printing cycle. This leaves a printable image on the blanket when it returns to the plate for the next impression. If the remaining image on the blanket and the new image printed by the plate are not exactly in register, a double image on the blanket results.

If there is no subsequent shift in register between plate and blanket, the double will print until all of the available ink on the first image (on the blanket) is removed. Because this image has a very limited supply of ink, ghosting is an intermittent problem that can last four or five impressions at the most. For the problem to continue longer, a new shift in register must occur.

Doubling between units may have been a problem in the past, but with today's inks it probably no longer occurs. To create the problem between units, enough ink printed by unit A must be backtrapped on the blanket of unit B to allow it to reprint on the web. With modern inks it is unlikely that backtrapping to this extent can occur.

Cause A: The plate cylinder (which is normally driven by a gear on the blanket cylinder) is trying to run ahead of the blanket cylinder. This situation is created when the blanket is packed to a greater diameter than that of the plate — a condition that occurs in many plants. The resulting greater circumference of the blanket tends to give it a greater surface speed than that of the plate. The tendency for greater blanket speed, resisted by the blanket-to-plate contact, creates forces causing intermittent register shifts.

Remedy 1:
Change the packing so that the plate is packed as high as possible and the blanket as low as possible.

Remedy 2:
Check bearer pressure and reset if necessary.

Cause B: Excessive play in the bearings or gears of plate and blanket cylinders.

Remedy:
Have press overhauled and replace worn parts. NOTE: If the doubling is from side to side, end play in either the plate or blanket cylinder could be the cause.

Cause C: Bearer pressure is low.

Remedy:
Reset bearers.

Trouble: **Paper is delaminated** in passing through the press printing units. Delamination occurs only on blanket-to-blanket web offset presses, and is more likely to occur where cylinder diameters are small. Delaminations are rough-edged, long-in-the-press-direction, single-sided flaws, as opposed to heat blisters, which are well defined, round or oval (not oriented to the press direction), and show on both sides of the web wherever they occur.

Cause: A web tends to wrap around any blanket that prints a solid. But if the solid is backed up by a solid of the same ink, the web tends to wrap on both blankets. This tendency produces internal shear, often strong enough to rupture the paper's fibrous structure.

How the web tends to cling to one blanket and then the other on a blanket-to-blanket web offset press.

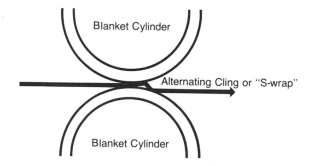

Blanket Cylinder

Alternating Cling or "S-wrap"

Blanket Cylinder

Delaminated web
resulting from sharp
flexing of web due to
alternating web wrap.

Remedy 1:
Reduce the tack of the ink. Delamination may be stopped
by softening the ink on one side only. This should prevent
the snapping back and forth.

Remedy 2:
Reduce the press speed. This will reduce the force required
to overcome the pull of the inks.

Remedy 3:
Increase tension to reduce the tendency of the web to wrap
on both blankets.

Remedy 4:
Try reversing the web. The wire side is usually more
resistant to delamination than the felt side. Printing the wire
side from the more critical form may help.

Remedy 5:
Install one or more grater rollers to deflect the web and
make it hug one of the blanket cylinders for an appreciable
distance beyond the impression line. In this way, the web

will not be free to snap back and forth between the two blankets.

NOTE 1: Some presses are designed with grater rollers to minimize web wrap in printing solids. On other presses, the upper and lower blanket cylinders are staggered or out of vertical alignment. Even though the web travel on staggered cylinder presses is straight through, the web automatically hugs the lower blanket, minimizing delamination.

NOTE 2: Delamination should not be confused with blistering of coated papers due to dryer heat. For blistering, see "Dryer and Chill Stand Troubles."

Trouble: **Rusting** of the plate cylinder destroys the trueness of the cylinder surface.

Cause: Seepage of water under the edges of the plate and soaking of the packing sheets.

Remedy 1:
Oil the back of printing plates; then lay on the required packing sheets, and oil again. This procedure also prevents creeping of the packing during printing.

Remedy 2:
Clean plate and blanket cylinder bodies at every change of plate and blanket; then wipe cylinder with an oily wiper cloth or other rust inhibitor.

Trouble: **Overheating** of the printing unit. Excessive evaporation of the heatset ink solvent takes place if printing units become too hot. Loss of solvent can unduly increase the ink's tack and cause picking, splitting, and tearing of the paper. Loss of solvent can also increase wrap on the blankets, web flutter, and misregister.

Cause A: The working of tacky offset inks on the roller surfaces in the inking system generates heat. Part of this heat is absorbed by the rollers and drums and raises their temperature. The air has some cooling effect, as does the evaporation of dampening water emulsified in the ink. In printing at high speeds, this cooling is not enough to prevent overheating of the printing unit.

Remedy 1:
Water-cool the ink drums (vibrators). Most modern presses are equipped to do this with thermostatic control of the cooling water. (See discussion of inker cooling in the introduction to this section.)

Remedy 2:
Chill the fountain solution by refrigeration or even by adding ice cubes to the fountain. This remedy is at best a stopgap measure.

Remedy 3:
If a web preheater is used, install one or more chill rolls to reduce the web temperature before the web enters the printing units.

Cause B: Excessive pressure between rollers in the inking system.

Remedy:
Check the alignment and pressure between the rollers and drums in the inking system to be sure the pressure is not excessive.

Cause C: Web preheater is heating the paper too much, thus increasing the temperature of the printing units and the ink.

Remedy 1:
Cut down on the preheating.

Remedy 2:
Install chill rolls following the web preheater.

Chill rolls after preheater on the press infeed are small and are driven by the web.

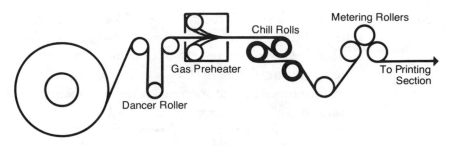

Cause D: Ultraviolet (UV) drying lamps overheat printing unit.

Remedy:
Check installation to see that proper heat carryoff is provided.

4 Ink Feed Troubles

Introduction   The inking system for each offset printing unit usually consists of an ink fountain, fountain roller, ductor roller, three or four metal or ebonite oscillating (vibrating) drums, four or more rubber intermediate rollers, and three or four rubber form rollers. The ink feed is controlled (1) by the setting of the flexible fountain blade which varies the amount of ink across the plate according to the demands of the plate and (2) by the rotation of the fountain roller or by the dwell of the ductor which governs the amount of ink fed to all areas. The ductor roller alternately contacts the fountain roller and an ink drum. The ductor transfers fresh ink to the drum. The ink is worked out to a thin, smooth film of printing consistency by the intermediate rollers and drums before reaching the form rollers. The form rollers then apply the ink to the plate according to plate requirements.

The conventional ink feed using the ductor roller is intermittent, and the reciprocal movement and changing of speed of the ductor roller produces noise and shock, especially on larger, high-speed presses. For this reason, continuous-feed inking systems are being developed and are in use on some high-speed news and publication presses.

In order to function properly, oscillating drums must be power driven at the same surface speed as the printing plate. The ductor, intermediate, and form rollers are driven by surface contact only. The fountain roller is driven either intermittently by means of an adjustable pawl and ratchet, or continuously through a gear from the press drive. The setting of the fountain blade and the movement of the fountain roller while in contact with the ductor determine the volume of ink delivered to the inking system and eventually to the paper. One inking system regulates the amount of ink by controlling the dwell of the ductor on the fountain roller by means of an adjustable cam.

Uniform distribution of ink around the rollers results from the differing diameters of the rollers and drums. Distribution over the length of the rollers is produced by oscillation of the vibrating drums, which is generally adjustable so that a differential ink feed to areas of greater or lesser ink demand can be maintained. Ink film thickness over the length of the rollers can be varied by adjusting the flexible fountain blade as mentioned previously. Lateral movement of the drums is reduced to a minimum when operating with two or more colors in a split fountain.

This section on "Ink Feed Troubles" is intended to give the web offset pressman a ready reference that will help him to: (1) avoid ink feed problems; (2) diagnose a problem quickly and correctly when it arises; (3) apply the proper remedy. Some of the remedies may not be possible under existing operating conditions—the press may not have the equipment or devices mentioned in the suggested remedy; it may not be possible to change the paper at the time; doctoring heatset inks should be avoided; a press mechanic may not be available in the plant, or he may not have the required equipment or parts on hand. For a chronic ink feed problem that can only be overcome with equipment or devices not available on the press, the suggested remedy may serve as a guide to management in its investigations of new equipment. Where the remedy suggests a major repair, this can serve as a signal to supervisory personnel that repair time must be scheduled. Where a remedy suggests changing paper or paper specifications, it is assumed that the paper supplier will be called in as soon as the trouble is identified as a paper problem; and correspondingly, the ink supplier when ink is concerned. For details on handling paper and paper complaints, see "Paper Troubles" section.

The principal troubles connected with the inking system are as follows:

Trouble: **Roller and blanket streaks** are always parallel to the axes of the rollers and cylinders. But, unlike gear streaks, they usually have no relationship to the pitch of the teeth of the cylinder drive gears. There may be only one streak or several. Streaks may or may not be spaced at equal intervals.

Typical cylinder and roller arrangement on a blanket-to-blanket press.

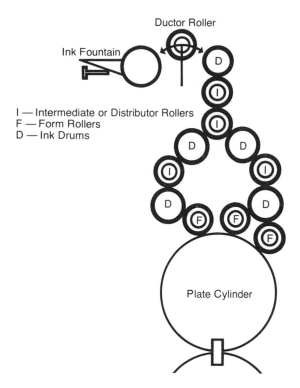

Ink Fountain

Ductor Roller

I — Intermediate or Distributor Rollers
F — Form Rollers
D — Ink Drums

Plate Cylinder

Cause A: One or more form rollers are set too hard against the plate. When they pass the cylinder gap, they strike the leading edge of the plate and bounce. This ruptures their ink films from end to end, producing a streak that is transferred to the plate after one revolution of the roller. Such streaks are worse if all form rollers are the same size and if more than one are set too hard against the plate. Streaks are most objectionable on background color tints.

Remedy:
Reset the form rollers to proper pressures against the plate and drum.

Cause B: Skidding form rollers, which can be caused by a roller being set with unequal pressure against its drum and the plate. The harder the setting, the greater the driving force and the slower the form roller is driven. So, if settings are unequal, the roller will skid on the surface where the setting is lighter, producing streaks. Skidding is more likely to occur if the rollers are glazed.

Remedy 1:
Reset the form rollers with equal pressures against the drums and plate.

Remedy 2:
Recondition the form rollers and drums to remove glaze. Glaze is due to accumulations of dried ink vehicle and gum not removed by ordinary wash-up solvents. Use one of the glaze-removing materials. Remove the form rollers, and scrub them and the drums with pumice powder and ink solvent to remove the glaze.

Cause C: Too much pressure and/or too little bearer pressure between cylinders. Such incorrect pressure can cause movement of the cylinder during printing when the gaps come together, and if the problem exists between the plate and blanket cylinders as illustrated here, streaks may form at points 1, 2, and 3. The problem can also occur between blanket cylinders, in which case the streak occurs in the plate-blanket nip.

Remedy:
Correct packing and/or bearer pressure (s).

Cause D: A loose and slipping blanket. Because of packing differences, the surface speeds of the plate and blanket are not always exactly equal. If the blanket is loose, it may tend to follow the plate and slip on the blanket cylinder. This slippage is intermittent, causing streaks. The greater the plate-to-blanket pressure, the worse the slippage.

How a loose offset blanket can slip on its cylinder and cause slurring and streaks.

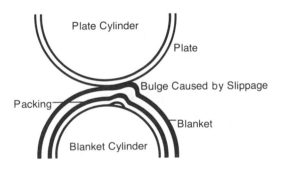

Remedy:
Tighten the blanket. Use the packing gauge to check the plate-to-blanket pressure. If too high, remove the excess packing.

Trouble: **Ink feeds unevenly.**

Cause A: Stripping of ink drums and/or rollers. This can result from (1) glazed drums or rollers or (2) using too much gum or phosphoric acid or both in the dampening solution. The rollers become preferentially wet by water and refuse to take and transfer ink. The result is inability to maintain color. Generally, metal drums are the more likely to strip; but the form rollers, too, can strip if they become glazed.

A stripped ink roller.

Remedy 1:
Wash up the press, using one of the glaze-removing wash-up methods.

Remedy 2:
If only the metal drums are stripping, wash the system free from ink, remove the form and intermediate rollers, and scrub the metal drums thoroughly with pumice powder and ink solvent.

Remedy 3:
If the rubber rollers strip, the glaze can be removed by

scrubbing with a 5% caustic soda (lye) solution and pumice powder. Caution: for this job, wear goggles, rubber gloves, and a rubber apron.

Remedy 4:
If rubber rollers strip, they can be reground in a lathe to remove the glaze, provided the grinding is done precisely.

Remedy 5:
Since the steel drums are most likely to strip, these can be removed and covered with ebonite or electroplated with copper. Both of these materials strongly resist stripping.

Cause B: Low spots in rollers preventing uniform contact between them or between form rollers and plate. The rubber rollers are more likely than the steel drums to have low spots.

Remedy:
Remove the defective rollers and have them reground, taking off enough material to make them absolutely true.

Cause C: Roller cores or spindles are bent.

Remedy:
Remove the defective rollers and have their coverings removed. Have the cores or spindles straightened before re-covering.

Cause D: The fountain blade has become bent or has worn unevenly and developed a scalloped edge. These conditions prevent accurate ink feed adjustment.

Remedy:
Obtain a new, straight fountain blade. When installing it, be sure the thumbscrews are backed off and that they turn freely. Use the thumbscrews and a feeler gauge to adjust the blade according to the press manufacturer's instructions, usually to a uniform clearance of 0.050 inch (1.27 millimeters). From this point, make further adjustments according to job requirements. Never force the blade against

the fountain roller, since doing so would cause uneven wear. When tightening the blade overall, start by turning the center screws and work toward the ends. When opening up the blade gap, start at both ends and work toward the center. This procedure will prevent the development of buckles or kinks in the blade.

Cause E: Dried ink or dirt has accumulated between the fountain blade and roller and is interfering with the ink feed.

Remedy:
Keep the blade and fountain roller clean at all times.

Cause F: The rubber at the ends of one or more rollers swells, peels, or blisters because the washup attachment is leaving ink and solvent to dry on the ends of the rollers. The result is poor inking along the sides of the plate.

Remedy:
When the machine washup is completed, always wipe the ends of the rollers and drums clean. Replace rollers that have become damaged.

Trouble: **Printing gradually loses density** or becomes grainy during run.

Cause A: Loss of printing pressure. A new blanket is packed to the proper height for adequate pressure, but the blanket becomes thinner under the continual rolling pressure. Both the plate-to-blanket and blanket-to-paper pressures decrease.

Remedy:
Use a packing gauge to check the heights of the plate and blanket with reference to the bearers. If there is not enough height to provide printing pressure, add packing under the blanket to bring it to the proper height.

Using a packing gauge to measure blanket height.
Courtesy of Baldwin-Gegenheimer Corp.

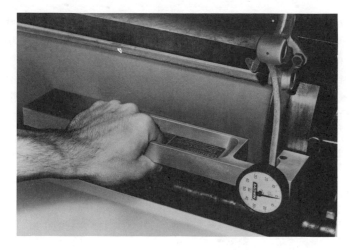

Cause B: Ink seems to "back away" from the fountain roller, causing ink feed to diminish. Actually, the ink simply sets up in the fountain and stops flowing down to the fountain roller.

Remedy 1:
Work the ink in the fountain frequently to keep it fluid.

Remedy 2:
Install a mechanical ink fountain agitator.

Mechanical ink agitator in ink fountain keeps ink semifluid and flowing.

Cause C: Ink builds, piles, or cakes on the roller surfaces and on the image areas of the plate and blanket. The ink fails to transfer properly, resulting in graininess or loss of density. Piling may be due to incompletely dispersed pigments or to the ink becoming waterlogged.

Remedy 1:
Check the degree of pigment dispersion in the ink by means of a fineness-of-grind gauge, or Grindometer (see GATF publication *What the Lithographer Should Know about Ink*). If the test shows many coarse particles or aggregates, have the ink reground.

Remedy 2:
Reduce the plate moisture to a minimum.

Remedy 3:
Add a small amount of suitable varnish to the ink, or get an ink that resists waterlogging. Consult your inkmaker.

Cause D: Ink rollers become fouled with lint and/or pick-outs from the paper. Ink on the plate and blanket images also becomes fouled. The material from the paper, being cellulose, absorbs water, becomes ink-repellent, and prevents the transfer of a continuous ink film.

Remedy 1:
Wash all possible ink off the press rollers with the washup attachment. Then handwash the rollers and drums to remove the lint and pick-outs.

Remedy 2:
Obtain a paper that has a lesser linting tendency and adequate pick resistance.

Remedy 3:
Soften the ink as much as possible to reduce its ability to pick up lint and particles of paper.

NOTE: When ultraviolet (UV) inks are being used, such ink can attack the bearing grease if it gets to it via the ink ductor roller, causing seizure and severe press damage. Keep bearing grease cups full.

Trouble: **Ghost images** appear in solids.

Cause: A narrow solid ahead of or behind a wider solid is robbing the form rollers of the ink needed to print full strength color in the corresponding area of the wider solid. Lateral distribution does not provide the extra ink in narrow sections needed to prevent ghosting.

Remedy 1:
Whenever possible, make layouts with solids well distributed.

Remedy 2:
Run a minimum of dampening solution.

Remedy 3:
Avoid running colors spare to produce tints. Consult inkmaker about obtaining a weaker color that can be run with a thicker ink film.

Remedy 4:
If possible, use opaque inks rather than transparent inks.

Remedy 5:
Cut down on the movement of the vibrating drums. This enables more ink to be confined to narrow areas of high demand and may in some cases reduce the ghosting.

5 Dampening Troubles

Introduction Web press dampening systems are essentially the same as those on sheetfed presses.

The conventional system consists of a water pan or fountain, fountain roller, ductor roller, distributing roller (vibrator), and one or two form dampening rollers.

The fountain roller is partially submerged in the fountain solution and rotates slowly. On modern web presses it has an independent variable-speed drive. It is usually made of stainless steel or chrome-plated steel and is run bare.

The conventional ductor is a fabric- or paper-covered roller that alternately contacts the fountain roller and the distributing roller. Its dwell on the fountain roller is adjustable and controls the amount of moisture fed to the dampeners. By varying the speed of the fountain roller, the water feed to the ductor is controlled, and fine adjustments are made possible.

Conventional
dampening system.

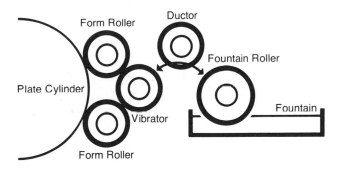

The water distributing roller is usually made of chrome-plated or stainless steel. It is constantly in contact with the dampening rollers and is driven so that its surface speed is the same as that of the press plate when packed to the specified height.

Historically, dampening systems have included one or more molleton-covered rollers. One of the problems created by these rollers is that it may require several minutes for the dampening system to adjust to a change in the dampening setting. In order to reduce the time required for the dampening system to adjust to a change, roller coverings with less water-storage capabilities have come into use. There is, however, a need for some storage capabilities because of surging, the change in the amount of water available to the plate at any given moment. Surging occurs because of the shortness in length of the dampening system and because of the intermittent action of the ductor. The problem of surging is greatest in a system that is run with bareback form and distributor rollers, and least with a system that has molleton covers on those rollers. In between are a number of combinations with varying storage capabilities. It should be remembered that there is a conflict between the need for a fast response and the need for uniform dampening.

Three methods of applying parchment paper covers on dampening rollers.

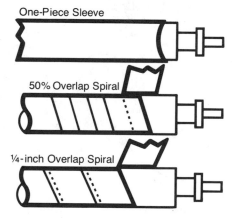

One-Piece Sleeve

50% Overlap Spiral

¼-inch Overlap Spiral

Another solution to the above problem has been the use of continuous-flow dampening systems. In these systems, a brush roll is used in two basically different ways. In one, the brush roll is used only as a means of transferring the fountain solution. It runs at relatively high speed and delivers a fine mist. Control of the solution is by means of a standard fountain roller and conventional water stops. The

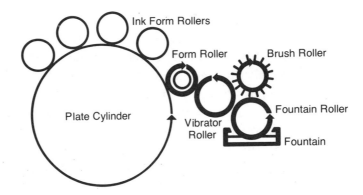

Continuous-flow dampening system with the brush used to transfer water from a conventional fountain roller.

brush roll systems of another type use the brush roll itself as the metering device. These brushes turn quite slowly and have a tendency to deliver water less uniformly than other systems. This problem can be overcome by adding a considerable amount of storage capability to the system, but this in turn produces a slow response to changes made by the pressman.

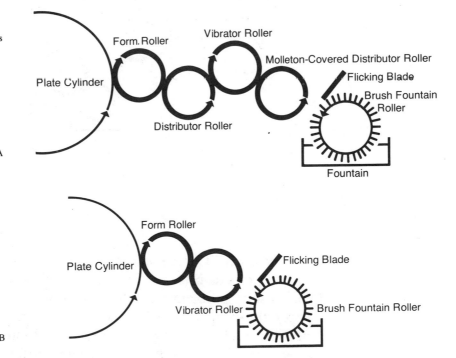

Two continuous-flow dampening systems with the brush used as the fountain roller. System A gives more uniform water feed because of the molleton-covered distributor.

Another continuous-flow dampening system that has proven to be very effective is the Dahlgren System. In this system, a rubber-covered metering roller runs in contact with a highly finished chromium-plated pan roller. These rollers are geared together and are driven by their own variable-speed motor. The pan roller is in constant contact with the first ink form roller, which is a special rubber roller substituted for the form roller. The chromium-plated pan roller transfers fountain solution directly to this special ink form roller, rather than to the plate. The rubber metering roller is adjustable against the pan roller and can be angled to better distribute the moisture on large presses where the ends of the rollers tend to receive too little moisture and dry up. The combination of variable-speed drive, pressure adjustment, and angling contribute to good water-feed control and distribution. In this, and similar systems becoming available, isopropyl alcohol replaces some of the water in the fountain solution being run.

The Dahlgren dampening system.

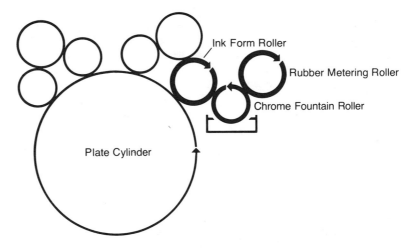

Ink Form Roller

Rubber Metering Roller

Chrome Fountain Roller

Plate Cylinder

This section on "Dampening Troubles" is intended to help the offset pressman: (1) avoid dampening problems; (2) diagnose a problem quickly and correctly when it arises; (3) apply the proper remedy. Some of the remedies may not be possible under existing operating conditions—the press may not have the equipment or devices mentioned in the suggested remedy; it may not be possible to change the paper at that time; doctoring heatset inks is not a simple thing to do; a press mechanic may not be available in the plant, or he may not have the required equipment or parts. For a chronic dampening problem that can only be overcome with unavailable equipment or devices, the suggested remedy may serve as a guide to management in its investigations of new equipment. Where the remedy suggests a major repair, this can serve as a signal to supervisory personnel that repair time must be scheduled. Where a remedy suggests changing paper or paper specifications, it is assumed that the paper supplier will be called in as soon as the trouble is identified as a paper problem; and correspondingly, the ink supplier when the ink is concerned. For details on handling paper and paper complaints, see the "Paper Troubles" section.

Proper plate dampening is essential to control the ink-water balance which, in turn, is essential to high quality printing. The following press troubles can result when this is not accomplished.

Trouble: **Dampening solution varies** from day to day.

Cause: The chemical composition of the water used for mixing dampening solutions changes periodically. Municipal water is required only to be safe for drinking. This does not guarantee that the water is chemically uniform from day to day or from season to season.

Remedy 1:
Switch to deep-well water if available.

Remedy 2:
Try using a commercial source for water. Spring water is usually nonchanging. If "distilled" water is used, it should be checked periodically.

Remedy 3:
Have installed a system for deionizing available water. To insure proper operation, such a system must be monitored on a regular basis.

Trouble:
Wash marks appear as weak areas extending back from the leading edges of solids.

Cause:
Too much dampening water; the excess is not being taken up by the ink.

Remedy:
Reduce the water feed. But if the water control is so critical as to leave little margin between wash marks and scumming, either the plate is too poorly desensitized or the ink is too water-repellent.

Trouble:
Snowflaky solids. Black solids are gray, and color solids are weak. Under a glass, solids appear uneven and full of tiny white specks.

Cause A:
Too much dampening water; the excess is taken up by the ink. Then, when the ink film is split, water droplets are exposed. These droplets prevent transfer of a uniform solid to the paper.

Remedy:
Reduce the water feed. If the ink on the rollers appears to be waterlogged (greatly shortened by the moisture), change to an ink that is more resistant to waterlogging.

Cause B:
Temperature of cooling water circulated through ink drums is too low—below 70°F (21°C). In humid weather, this can cause condensation of moisture on the ink drums and promote emulsification and waterlogging.

Remedy:
Raise the temperature of the cooling water.

Trouble: **Scum streaks** around the cylinder.

Cause A: Dirty or worn dampener or ductor roller covers, which can prevent uniform dampening across the press.

Remedy 1:
Wash dampener or ductor roller covers to remove ink accumulation. Replace threadbare roller covers.

Remedy 2:
Try parchment paper dampener covers. These covers require special rollers.

Cause B: Greasing of the fountain roller or distributing roller. Greasing can prevent uniform dampening across the press, because greasy rollers cannot hold a continuous film of water.

Remedy:
Scrub fountain and distributing rollers with powdered pumice and naphtha; then etch them, drying the etch down.

Cause C: Nonuniform pressure of dampening rollers against the plate, causing uneven wear.

Remedy 1:
Reset dampening rollers, making sure the pressure is uniform from end to end. After setting, the rollers should never be reversed end for end.

Remedy 2:
Check dampeners for trueness. If a spindle or stock is bent, it should be straightened and the roller re-covered.

Trouble: **Scum streaks across the plate** are usually due to lack of sufficient moisture or to excessive plate wear.

Cause: Bouncing dampening rollers. Rollers are set too hard against the plate and bounce when they strike the leading edge of the plate. The bump causes rapid wear of the plate's front edge, producing a scum streak.

Remedy:
Reset the dampening rollers to the proper pressure to eliminate bounce.

NOTE: For other causes of scum streaks across the plate, see Section 4, "Ink Feed Troubles."

Trouble: **Water streaks** appear in the printing.

Cause: Ductor roller striking the distributor roller, producing a bead of water.

Remedy:
Adjust ductor to lighter contact with distributor.

Trouble: **Plate tends to develop a general scum** after job has been running for some time.

Cause: Insufficient acid or gum or both in the fountain solution.

Remedy:
Reformulate dampening solution.

NOTE: For other causes of plate scumming, see Section 6, "Plate Troubles."

Trouble: **Halftones sharpen** and highlights are lost during run.

Cause: Too much acid in the fountain solution is undercutting the printing areas.

Remedy:
Once highlight dots have been lost, they cannot be brought back. Remake the plate and adjust the pH value of the fountain solution.

NOTE: Other causes of image failure are discussed in Section 6, "Plate Troubles."

Trouble: **Fiber-shaped white spots** appearing in printed solids result from adhesion of cellulose fibers to the plate or blanket. Such fibers absorb moisture until they become saturated, after which they repel ink.

Enlargement of a printed area showing lint.

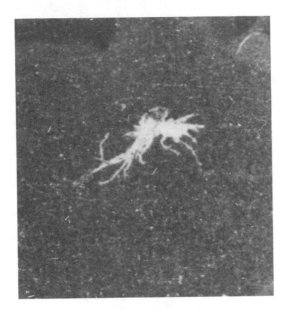

Cause A: Lint, fluff, or whiskers picked up from the paper or board. This is a paper trouble.

Remedy:
See Section 8, "Paper Troubles."

Cause B: Fibers released from fabric- or paper-covered dampening roller covers. These covers eventually shed their nap fibers as a result of wear or mildew. Nap fibers can be distinguished from paper fibers since nap fibers are generally from two to four times as long. Nap fibers can also be identified by laboratory tests.

Remedy 1:
Re-cover the dampener and ductor rollers.

Remedy 2:
Use parchment paper dampener covers, which are replaced

frequently and do not shed fibers. These covers require special rollers.

Trouble:	**Plate image wears.**

Cause A: Too much gum in the fountain water.

Remedy:
Re-etch the plate and rub up the image areas with press ink. Turn off water fountain supply, drain the fountain, and fill with plain tap water. If image comes back, replace the tap water with a fountain solution containing less gum arabic; if not, see Cause B. See also Section 6, "Plate Troubles."

NOTE: When ultraviolet (UV) inks are used, they can more readily dissolve the image areas from the plate.

Cause B: Too much acid in the fountain water. This condition is indicated by roller stripping or by the tendency of the plate to scum prior to loss of image.

Remedy:
Replace fountain solution with one having a higher pH value.

Trouble: **Plate scums or tints.**

Cause: Fountain water is extracting an emulsifying or sensitizing agent from the paper coating. This condition is proved if substitution of another paper stops the tinting.

Remedy 1:
Stiffen the ink as much as possible or try a stiffer ink. Consult your inkmaker.

Remedy 2:
Avoid use of a wetting agent in the fountain solution.

Remedy 3:
Get another paper.

Trouble: **Ink fails to dry rub-resistant.**

Cause A: Too much acid in the dampening solution. Acid can retard or prevent drying of inks that contain drying oil and drier.

Remedy:
Increase the fountain solution pH.

Cause B: For ultraviolet (UV) drying, not enough exposure to UV for the ink film thickness.

Remedy:
Increase UV exposure or decrease ink film thickness.

6 Plate Troubles

Introduction

The lithographic press plate is different from other printing plates in that the litho plate is planographic. That is, the image and non-image areas are essentially on the same level; the image areas are not raised as in letterpress, nor depressed as in gravure printing. The image areas are simply ink-receptive areas surrounded by water-receptive non-image areas. When moistened, the water-receptive areas refuse to take ink, while the image areas repel the water.

The printing cycle consists, therefore, of (1) dampening the plate's non-image areas; (2) inking the image areas; and (3) transferring the ink from the image areas to the blanket, from which the image is "offset" onto the paper, paperboard, metal, plastic, or other substrate.

On the first metal lithographic plates, the image areas were drawn by hand with crayon or tusche, or were hand-transferred from ink images on stones. Later, printers found that the image areas could be produced photographically by using negatives or positives in conjunction with light-sensitive coated plates. This method greatly improved the quality of halftones and, today, "photolithographic" methods of platemaking are used exclusively.

Surface Plates: Surface plates are made by covering a clean metal plate with a light-sensitive coating, exposing to light through a line or halftone film, developing to remove unwanted coating from the non-image areas, and desensitizing the non-image areas.

Cross section of a surface plate.

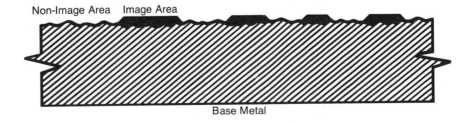

Non-Image Area   Image Area

Base Metal

There are three types of surface plates in general use:
(1) ungrained aluminum plates sensitized with photopolymers
and diazo compounds, called "presensitized plates," which
are purchased ready for exposure; (2) grained aluminum
plates sensitized with diazo compounds by the lithographer,
called "wipe-on" plates; (3) anodized plates, grained or
ungrained, presensitized with photopolymers and diazo
monomers.

Presensitized aluminum plates produce high quality. Wipe-on
plates also produce high quality and good plate life. A
presensitized plate that has been baked will have increased
durability of the image, thereby improving press
performance.

Deep-Etch Plates: Deep-etch plates are made by coating a
clean aluminum or stainless steel plate with bichromated
gum arabic, exposing it to light through a line or halftone
positive, developing to remove unexposed coating from the
image areas, "deep-etching" the image areas, applying lacquer
and ink to the image areas, removing the bichromated gum
stencil, and desensitizing the non-image area.

Cross section of a
deep-etch plate.

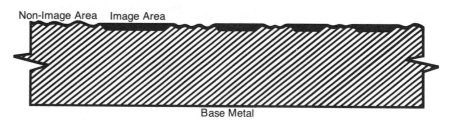

Non-Image Area   Image Area

Base Metal

Actually, the deep-etching is less than 0.0003 inch (0.007
millimeter), too shallow to produce appreciable image
depression. All that is necessary, really, is to remove enough
metal to assure absolute cleanness.

In the case of aluminum plates, the image areas are
generally copperized to increase the adhesion of lacquer and
ink.

Bimetal and Multimetal Plates: Plates of more than one metal are distinguished by having image and non-image areas differentiated by different metals—chromium, stainless steel, or aluminum for the non-image areas and copper for the image areas.

There are two general types of these plates:
(1) "Negative-working" (bimetal) plates, in which copper is electroplated on stainless steel or aluminum. These plates are coated with bichromated gum arabic, exposed through negatives, developed to bare the copper in the non-image areas, then etched to remove the copper from these areas, leaving copper on the printing areas. (2) "Positive-working" plates, in which copper is electroplated on aluminum or iron base plate, followed by a thin layer of electroplated chromium. These are coated with bichromated gum arabic, exposed through positives, developed to bare the chromium in the image areas, leaving chromium on the non-image areas. Such plates are often called "trimetal" plates.

Cross section of a bimetal plate.

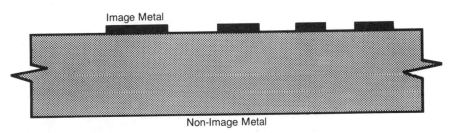

Cross section of a trimetal plate.

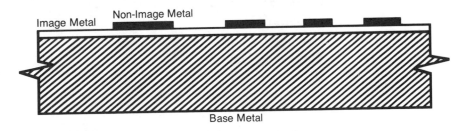

Presensitized multimetal plates are available.

Paper Plates: There are two general types of paper plates: direct-image plates upon which the image is produced by typewriting or printing, and presensitized plates upon which the image is produced photographically. Such plates are used extensively on offset duplicators, but are available in commercial sizes up to about 40 inches by 54 inches (1.0 meter by 1.4 meters). These plates are primarily for black-and-white printing and are not recommended for multicolor work.

Paper plates are unsuitable for use on web offset presses because of their short printing life and tendency to stretch, especially when dampened. The principal plates used in web offset printing are wipe-on aluminum, copperized aluminum deep-etch, bimetal or trimetal, and anodized presensitized negative and positive plates.

Cost and Longevity: There is considerable variation in the cost of these different plates, and the length of the run usually determines which one is selected. Their approximate printing lives are as follows:

Type of Plate	Length of Run
Presensitized Paper	up to 5,000
Direct-Image Paper	up to 10,000
Presensitized Aluminum	20,000 - 50,000
Wipe-on	50,000 - 100,000
Copperized Aluminum Deep-Etch	300,000 - 500,000
Baked Presensitized	500,000 - 1,000,000
Bimetal or Trimetal	1,000,000 +
Brass Plate	1,000,000 +

Regardless of type of plate being used, plate life and print quality depend both on correct plate preparation and on proper plate handling on the press. Rollers must be properly set; cylinder packings and pressures must be correct; press crews must gum up and wash out plates properly. For

details on methods of making lithographic plates, see the
GATF book *Offset Lithographic Platemaking*.

This section on "Plate Troubles" is intended to give the
web offset pressman a ready reference that will help him to:
(1) minimize plate troubles on the press; (2) diagnose a
problem quickly and correctly when it arises; (3) apply the
proper remedy. Some of the remedies may not be possible
under existing operating conditions — the plate-bending jig
may not have a vacuum hold-down; the plates may come
from an outside supplier; it may not be possible to change
the paper at the time; doctoring heatset inks should be
avoided. For a chronic plate problem that involves
equipment, management must study the economic feasibility
of changing or modifying the equipment. Where a chronic
problem involves platemaking techniques, supervisory
personnel must get together with the platemaking
department or the plate supplier to solve and eliminate the
problem. Where a remedy suggests changing paper or paper
specifications, it is assumed that the paper supplier will be
called in as soon as the trouble is identified as a paper
problem; and correspondingly, the ink supplier when ink is
concerned. For details on handling paper and paper
complaints, see the "Paper Troubles" section. The pH of the
fountain solution and percent of alcohol (if used) should be
monitored by a quality control system.

The following are the principal plate troubles likely to occur
on web offset presses:

Trouble: **Plate image under developing ink cannot be washed
out** with Lithotine or comparable product.

Cause A: Gum has dried over all or part of the image areas,
preventing solvent from contacting and dissolving the
developing ink.

Remedy:
Wet-wash the plate. For steps of procedure for wet-washing
a plate see illustration.

With the ink and dampener rollers up, wash the plate with clean water and a sponge.

While the plate is still damp with water, wash the ink off the image using a soft cloth and Lithotine solvent. Go over the plate twice with the solvent. Don't let the plate dry.

Wash the solvent and dissolved ink off the plate with clean water and a sponge. Go over the plate twice.

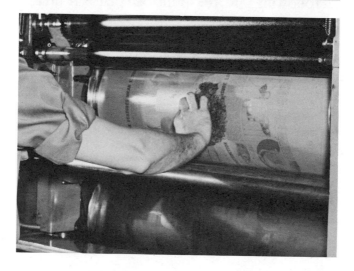

While the plate is still damp with water, start the press and drop the ink rollers. When image is fully inked, drop the dampeners, and resume or start printing.

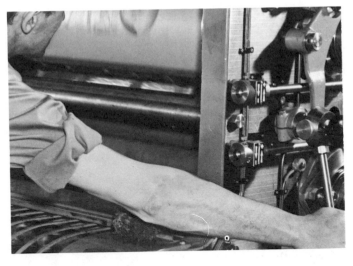

Cause B: Developing ink has dried hard on the image areas, and Lithotine or comparable product will not remove it.

Remedy 1:
Wash the plate with a solvent formulated for removal of dried ink, such as a 50-50 mixture of xylol and ethyl acetate or xylol and butyl acetate. This must be done with the plate under gum. When the ink has been removed, put the plate under asphaltum.

Remedy 2:
Have platemaker use a developing ink that will not dry hard, or have him put plates under asphaltum.

Trouble: **Plate refuses to roll up properly.**

Cause A: Gum has dried over all or part of the image area, preventing solvent from contacting and dissolving the developing ink.

Remedy 1:
Wet-wash the plate. (See illustration.)

Remedy 2:
Get a new plate. Before gumming up plates, be sure they are fully inked up.

Cause B: Developing ink has dried on the image areas and cannot be washed out.

Remedy 1:
Wash the plate with a solvent formulated for removal of dried ink, such as a 50-50 mixture of xylol and ethyl acetate or xylol and buytl acetate. This must be done with the plate under gum. When the ink has been removed, put the plate under asphaltum.

Remedy 2:
Wash plate with hot water.

Remedy 3:
Lacquer the plate with a wipe-on lacquer.

Remedy 4:
Have platemaker use a developing ink that will not dry hard, or have him put plates under asphaltum.

NOTE: For detailed instructions on applying developing ink, see GATF publication *Offset Lithographic Platemaking*.

Trouble: **Plate under asphaltum cannot be washed out** with water.

Cause A: Asphaltum was put on too thick. Water cannot penetrate the asphaltum and dissolve the gum.

Remedy 1:
Wet-wash the plate. (See illustration.) Then roll the plate up with ink.

Remedy 2:
If the image areas do not roll up properly, get a new plate.

NOTE: For detailed instructions on putting plates under asphaltum, see GATF publication *Offset Lithographic Platemaking*.

Cause B: Too thin a gum film on the plate. When applied, the asphaltum penetrates the gum.

Remedy 1:
Wet-wash the plate. (See illustration.)

Remedy 2:
Get a new plate.

NOTE: For detailed instructions on gumming up plates, see GATF publication *Offset Lithographic Platemaking*.

Cause C: Gum on the plate was not thoroughly dry when asphaltum was applied. Asphaltum penetrates the gum.

Remedy 1:
Wet-wash the plate. (See illustration.)

Remedy 2:
On future plates, make sure gum is thoroughly dry.

Trouble: **Non-image areas become greasy** or scummy.

Cause A: Dirty or worn dampener covers.

Remedy:
Clean or re-cover the dampening rollers. Wet-washing may save the plate.

NOTE: To remove scum from bimetal plates, see the topic "Bimetal Plate Goes Blind" in this section.

Cause B: Running too much ink on halftones. Excess ink spreads over the edge of the halftone dots onto non-image areas; eventually the non-image areas become sensitized.

Remedy:
Run the ink as stiff and spare as is practical.

Cause C: Wear of plate due to piling of abrasive material from the paper on the blanket.

Remedy:
Change to a better paper.

Cause D: Oxidation of aluminum plates. Oxidation scum appears as a multitude of fine, sharp dots. Scum is most likely to appear in areas which have stood opposite moist dampening rollers. Oxidation happens if (1) a wet plate dries too slowly, (2) a plate is stored in a damp area either before processing or while being held for a rerun, or (3) the press is stopping during a run before the plates have dried.

Enlargement showing oxidation (ink-dot scum) on an aluminum plate.

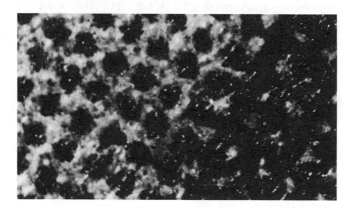

Remedy:
Care should be taken in handling aluminum plates. Plates should be stored in a dry place. During platemaking, dry them quickly under a fan. When shutting down the press, allow it to idle with form and dampening rollers off until the plate or plates are dry.

Cause E: Improper functioning of dampening or inking rollers, or of both, which results in scum streaks either horizontal or around the cylinder. These troubles are not the fault of the plate.

Remedy:
Check pressure, cleanliness, trueness, and general condition of inking and dampening rollers. Remedy according to the suggestions given in "Ink Feed Troubles: Roller and Blanket Streaks" and "Dampening Troubles: Scum Streaks."

Cause F: Plate was not properly desensitized when made.

Remedy:
Try re-etching and gumming the plate on the press. Before doing this, be sure the image areas are well protected with ink. Also make sure to dry the etch down thoroughly before washing it off. If this does not remove the scum, try wet-washing the plate and rolling the image up with ink before etching and gumming it.

Cause G: Ink is too soft or greasy.

Remedy:
Stiffen the ink. Call the ink supplier for advice.

Cause H: Abrasive pigment particles or aggregates in the ink.

Remedy:
Have the ink reground or replaced with a better ink.

Cause I: Abrasive material picked up from the paper surface by the blanket.

Remedy:
Reduce the plate-to-blanket pressures to a minimum on blanket-to-blanket presses; if an impression cylinder is involved, check impression to paper. If possible, change to another paper.

Cause J: Counter-etching in multicolor printing, sometimes called "secondary scumming." This condition can occur on any unit of a multicolor press except the first. What can happen, for example, is that the printed ink from the first unit is picked up by the offset blanket of the second unit so that the first ink runs in contact with the non-image areas of the second plate. If these areas are sensitized by the first-unit ink, a scum will be developed on these areas. This scum will print over the first-unit areas on the press sheets, changing the values of these areas. This type of scumming is usually less troublesome with the finer-grained plates. Secondary scumming seldom occurs when running bimetal plates.

Remedy 1:
If poor plate desensitization is suspected, re-etch and gum up the scumming plate.

Remedy 2:
Increase the acid and gum in the fountain water on the plate giving trouble.

Remedy 3:
Run the ink more sparely on the preceding unit. If necessary, use an ink with greater color strength.

Cause K: Greasy metering roller in Dahlgren-type dampening system.

Remedy:
Clean metal rollers in the system.
(Consult supplier for recommended procedure.)

Trouble: **Non-image areas print an overall tint** although plate is not greasy.

Cause A: The non-image areas of the plate have not been well desensitized due to incomplete removal of plate coating. To check this, wash all tint off the plate, polish part of a blank area with a scotch stone or snakeslip, and give the entire plate a light etch. If, on resuming the run, the polished area remains clean while the surrounding area tints, the cause is residual coating. If all areas continue to tint, the cause is either the paper (see Cause B) or a breakdown of the ink (see Cause C). If the test indicates the presence of a residual coating, proceed as follows:

Remedy 1:
Try adding more fountain etch, but do not reduce the pH value of the fountain solution too much or ink drying time may be affected.

Remedy 2:
Send the plate back to the plateroom for further treatment. See plate posttreatment in the GATF publication *Offset Lithographic Platemaking*.

Remedy 3:
In the case of an aluminum deep-etch plate with residual coating, wash the plate with the following solution:

Oxalic acid	6 ounces (0.177 liter)
Hot water	8 ounces (0.236 liter)

Apply with a rag or sponge, then wash off with water and proceed to print.

Cause B: An emulsifying or sensitizing agent is being extracted from the paper coating. This is a likely possibility if the substitution of another paper stops the tinting.

Remedy 1:
Stiffen the ink as much as possible, or try another ink. Consult with the inkmaker.

Remedy 2:
Avoid using any wetting agent in the fountain water.

Remedy 3:
Use another paper.

Cause C: The ink is not sufficiently water-resistant and is broken down by the fountain solution. In single-color presswork, if changing the paper does not stop the tinting, the trouble is either with the ink or the plate. In multicolor presswork, if all the inks are tinting, the cause is most likely the paper (see Cause B). If one or two inks are tinting while the others are printing clean, ink or plate trouble is indicated.

Remedy:
Consult inkmaker with regard to stiffening the ink or replacing the ink.

NOTE: Inks designed for large or high-speed presses are likely to break down and tint when run on small presses at low speed, because of the low tack of the ink.

Trouble: **Plate fails to print full-strength color.**

Cause A: Image lacks ink affinity.

      Remedy:
      Wet-wash the plate. (See illustration.)

Cause B: Ink is too short or is waterlogged, and it is piling on the rollers, plate, and blanket.

      Remedy 1:
      Cut down fountain water to a minimum.

      Remedy 2:
      Lengthen the ink by adding a suitable varnish. Consult the inkmaker.

Cause C: Plate is starting to go blind.

      Remedy:
      See the topic "Image Goes Blind" in this section.

Trouble: **Image goes blind.**

Cause A: Too much gum in the fountain solution.

      Remedy:
      Re-etch the plate and rub up the image areas with press ink. Drain the fountain solution and replace with plain tap

water. If image comes back, replace the tap water with a fountain solution containing less gum arabic; if not, see remaining causes for "Image Goes Blind."

NOTE: When ultraviolet (UV) inks are used, they can more readily dissolve the image areas from the plate.

Cause B: Too much acid in the fountain solution. The excess acidity indicated by roller stripping or by tendency of the plate to scum prior to loss of image.

Remedy:
Drain fountain solution and replace with one having a higher pH value.

Cause C: Ink is too short and lacks water resistance.

Remedy:
Rub up the image areas. Consult ink supplier about how to lengthen the ink. If necessary, have fresh ink made.

Cause D: Plate-to-blanket pressure is too great, causing plate wear. This condition may be due to a swollen or embossed blanket.

Remedy:
Correct the plate-to-blanket pressure. Use packing gauge to check plate-to-blanket pressure. If blanket is badly embossed, replace it.

Cause E: Deep-etch plate was not completely developed. A thin film of gum still remains on the image areas. Eventually this gum takes water and releases the lacquer. The image becomes grainy, spotty, or blind.

Remedy:
None. Have the plate remade.

NOTE: Sulfur compounds cause blinding of copper images. Sulfur should never be used in connection with copper-image plates.

Trouble: **Bimetal plate goes blind.**

Cause A: The copper image on a chromium-copper or aluminum-copper plate has become desensitized. This could be caused by an accumulation of gum in the ink, or by sulfur or a sulfur compound.

Remedy:
Rub up the image areas with ink and dilute phosphoric or nitric acid—12 ounces to a gallon (94 milliliters to a liter) of water. Wash off the acid, etch the plate, and proceed to print.

CAUTION: This treatment should not be used on copperized aluminum plates, since chemically deposited copper is not sufficiently resistant to acids.

NOTE: Sulfur compounds cause blinding of copper images. Sulfur should never be used in connection with copper-image plates.

Cause B: The copper image on a stainless steel-copper plate has become desensitized.

Remedy:
Rub up the image areas with ink and a 2% sulfuric acid solution—2½ ounces concentrated sulfuric acid to a gallon (20 milliliters to a liter) of water. Wash off the acid, etch the plate, and proceed to print.

CAUTION: In making the 2% sulfuric acid solution, always add the acid to the water. Adding water to concentrated sulfuric acid could cause spattering and injury to the eyes and skin.

NOTE 1: Sulfur compounds cause blinding of copper images. Sulfur should never be used in connection with copper-image plates.

NOTE 2: The above acid treatments not only resensitize the copper image areas of bimetal plates but also remove scum from the non-image areas. However, plates should be re-etched to keep scum from coming back.

Trouble: **Halftones print grainy** or sandy.

Cause A: Deep-etch plate is not completely developed. Incomplete development could be due to overexposure or to dark reaction of the bichromated gum coating.

Remedy:
None. Have the plate remade.

Cause B: Coarse or uneven plate grain.

Remedy:
None. Have plate remade with finer, more uniform grain.

Cause C: Too much fountain solution. Water emulsifies in the ink and shortens or waterlogs it. Droplets of this emulsified water tend to wet the paper and prevent the ink from laying on the paper uniformly.

Remedy:
Cut down the dampening moisture. If plate then tends to scum, chances are that the plate was not desensitized properly. To remedy this scumming, try re-etching and gumming the plate on the press. Before doing this, be sure the image areas are well protected with ink. Also make sure to dry the etch thoroughly before washing it off. If this does not remove the scum, try wet-washing the plate and rolling the image up with ink before etching and gumming.

Crack at bend of an aluminum plate.

Trouble: **Aluminum plate cracks in bend** at front or back edge.

Cause: Plate is not mounted correctly and is not uniformly snug on the cylinder. This produces flexing at the bends. A correctly fitted plate will not crack.

Remedy 1:
Make sure when the plate edges are initially bent that the plate is held tightly so it cannot slip in the bending jig. A vacuum back on the jig helps to prevent slippage. When mounting the plate on the plate cylinder, be sure that the edges are pulled down tight so that there is no bulging and that the plate is uniformly snug on the cylinder.

Remedy 2:
Punch a small round hole at each end of the crack. This procedure can usually keep a crack from spreading until a new plate is made.

Remedy 3:
Check packing length. Short packing can also cause cracking.

NOTE: Mylar-backed aluminum plates that resist cracking and the spreading of cracks are available commercially. They allow time to make new plates without shutting down the press.

Trouble: **Plate cracks on front or back edge** during press run.

Cause A: Grain of metal plate wrong way on cylinder.

    Remedy:
    Check grain of metal with platemaker.

Cause B: Plates not drawn to cylinder tightly.

    Remedy:
    Plate too long around cylinder: check clamps for dried ink and adjustment; check size of plate with press specs.

Cause C: Thermal overbaking has made metal brittle.

    Remedy:
    Have platemaker check thermal baking specs with manufacturer.

Trouble: **Plate cracks in the middle** of its back edge.

Cause: Plate is pinched in the center, weakening the metal at that point and causing the plate to crack.

    Remedy 1:
    When bending edge, make sure the plate is squarely in the bending jig and the bending bar is straight.

    Remedy 2:
    Check for smooth, even bending without buckles or waves that will cause stress areas and potential breaking points during running.

Trouble: **Packing creeps** under plate during run.

Cause: Slipping of packing sheets on each other or on the cylinder. Slippage results in wrinkles that cause the plate to bulge, thus increasing pressures and causing plate wear.

Remedy 1:
Coat the back of the plate and the cylinder with a thin film of oil before applying the packing sheets and mounting the plate. This procedure also prevents rusting of the cylinder.

Remedy 2:
Apply several stripes of grease to the back of the plate to hold the packing in place.

Remedy 3:
Paste the leading edges of packing sheets together when using more than one sheet under the plate.

Remedy 4:
Fasten the packing sheets to the plate with an adhesive such as contact cement.

Trouble: **Losing image** on presensitized plate.

Cause: Automatic blanket wash solvents affect image area of some unbaked plates.

Remedy 1:
Use less-strong solvent, or hand-wash blankets when possible, being careful not to splash solvent on plates. Have new plate made.

Remedy 2:
Have plates baked before running. Doing so makes image areas impervious to solvents.

Trouble: **Presensitized plate slow to roll up.**

Cause: Some boxed presensitized plates are naturally slow to roll up. The thermal gum may have been applied too thick.

Remedy:
Wash out with manufacturer's plate cleaner or phosphoric acid solution—6 fluid ounces per gallon (50 milliliters per liter) of water.

Trouble: **Presensitized plate scums.**

Cause: Dirty dampeners, incorrect pH of fountains.

Remedy:
Wash out with manufacturer's plate cleaner and roll up. If cleaner not available, use phosphoric acid solution—6 fluid ounces per gallon (50 milliliters per liter) of water.

NOTE: Materials used on web presses using presensitized plates should be tightly controlled, along with their method of use.

Trouble: **Brass plates slow to roll up.**

Cause: New brass plates tend to be slow to roll up.

Remedy:
Wash with 2% sulfuric acid solution. While plate is still wet, drop rollers and roll up plate. If still slow to roll up, use pumice powder with the sulfuric acid solution, then wash off with water sponge, and drop rollers.

Trouble: **Surface of plate becomes scratched** from front to back edge, in a straight line, in a manner commonly called "Railroad Tracking."

Cause A: Small metal particles embedded in ink form rollers.

Remedy:
Remove and check all ink forms; scrub if necessary.

Cause B: Loose metal particles release from plate surface or edges.

Remedy:
Check plate surface and check edges for loose filing before mounting plates.

Cause C: On web presses using steel shafts in core of paper rolls, filings attach to web and transfer up to ink rollers.

Remedy:
See press specs regarding static controls.

Cause D: With conventional dampeners, hard or dry ink scratches surface of plate.

Remedy:
See "Offset Blanket Troubles" section.

7 Offset Blanket Troubles

Introduction   The most commonly used offset blankets consist of three or four plies of long-staple cotton fabric laminated together by means of a special rubber adhesive and then coated with a rubber compound on one side. The thickness of the rubber coating varies (depending on the manufacturer) from about 0.012 to 0.020 inch (0.3 to 0.5 millimeter), but the overall thickness of the blanket is about 0.065 inch (1.7 millimeters) for three-ply blankets and 0.075 inch (1.9 millimeters) for four-ply blankets. The exact thickness is not important, but individual blankets should be uniform in thickness. Accepted thickness variance is $\pm$ 0.001 inch (0.025 millimeter). Offset blankets are also made two-ply and five-ply when required.

Cross section of a four-ply offset blanket.

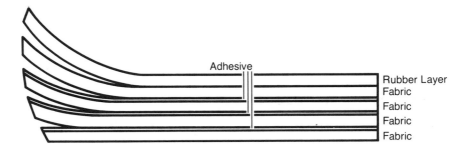

An offset blanket is wrapped around its cylinder and held under sufficient tension to prevent slippage on the cylinder under the rolling pressure of impression. The amount of tension can vary considerably since it is applied manually, but the average tension is estimated to be about 50 pounds per inch (880 grams per millimeter) of width. When a new blanket is installed, this tension plus the rolling-out effect of the impression may cause some stretching and necessitate the tightening of the blanket at intervals to take up the slack.

Another effect on the combined tension and rolling impression is the reduction in thickness of a new blanket during the first few thousand impressions. If the blanket thickness is measured with a micrometer, and the calculated thickness of packing is added to give 0.003 or 0.004 inch (0.08 or 0.10 millimeter) of impression, the impression may no longer be good after a few thousand revolutions. Checking with a packing gauge may show that the blanket has been compressed .002 (0.05 millimeter) or more and needs additional packing to receive a good impression from the plate.

The rubber layer, or printing surface, of the blanket was originally made from natural rubber. Today, the printing surface is made principally of synthetic rubber, because it is less oil-absorbent and therefore less susceptible to swelling, embossing, and the development of tackiness and glaze. In fact, tackiness of blankets has almost ceased to be a problem.

However, glazing of the blanket can occur by accumulation of dried ink, gum, and paper coating on the surface of the blanket or by surface oxidation. Causes of oxidation are bichromatic fountain solutions, heat, short-wavelength light, and ozone. A glazed blanket fails to transfer ink properly. Printing quality is restored by the removal of the glaze through scrubbing with a pumice and a solvent. When in good condition, the blanket surface has a soft, velvety feel, whereas rubbing a glazed blanket with the finger produces a "chattery" sensation.

There are two types of blankets commonly in use: the conventional blanket and the compressible blanket. The surface rubber layer on neither type of blanket is compressible; the surface is displaced during impression. This causes bulges to form outside the nip which may, under excessive pressure, lead to dot slur and contribute to premature wearing of presensitized or wipe-on plates.

The compressible blanket contains compressible layers underneath the surface rubber. The rubber-coated surface of the blanket is of a reduced thickness. Packing is less critical with their use. They are more smash-resistant, and they print with greater fidelity.

Packing requirements will vary depending on the type of blanket that is used. Assuming that present conditions require a pressure of 190 pounds per square inch (134 grams per square millimeter), a squeeze of about 0.003 inch (0.08 millimeter) will be needed with a conventional blanket to supply the desired pressure. With a compressible blanket, a squeeze of 0.005 inch (0.12 millimeter) will be needed to supply the equivalent pressure. This is shown in the illustration.

Comparison of squeeze required to obtain equal pressures for printing.

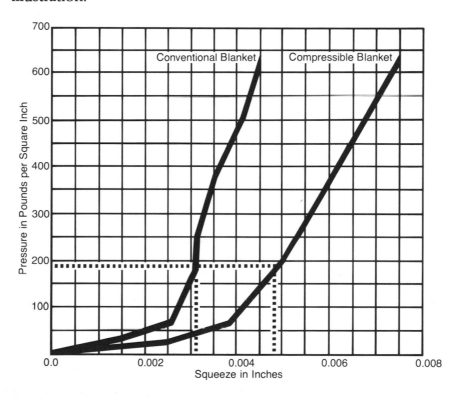

Virtually all problems that are definitely traced to the blanket arise from (1) incompatibility of blanket and ink, (2) improper mounting and packing of the blanket, and (3) improper treatment of the blanket when first put on the press or during printing. Blankets are available to match almost any ink-paper combination. However, it is imperative that the blanket supplier be fully advised of the particular ink and paper characteristics so that he can make the best possible recommendations. If a change is made in either ink or paper, the blanket supplier should again be consulted. This does not mean that the blanket can be depended upon to reduce problems caused by an unusual ink-paper-plate-fountain solution combination. Even with an ideal balancing of ink, paper, plate, fountain solution, and blanket, the blanket must be properly treated and handled. Here it is wise to consult the blanket and solvent suppliers, to assure best possible results.

Blanket manufacturers, solvent manufacturers, and GATF have published considerable information and detailed procedures on resting blankets to increase their useful life. Some pressrooms follow these procedures, but others believe in keeping a blanket on the press until it fails to produce quality printing, then discarding it. Which procedure is best in a particular plant can only be determined by cost studies of both procedures over a reasonable length of time.

It is hoped that this section, "Offset Blanket Troubles," will give the web offset pressman a ready reference to help him: (1) avoid troubles due to blankets and blanket handling; (2) quickly and correctly diagnose a trouble when it arises; (3) apply the proper remedy.

Following are some troubles that originate with offset blankets:

Trouble: **Printed impression** gradually loses sharpness or solidity.

Cause A: Blanket subsides or becomes thinner under the printing pressure. This trouble generally occurs with a new blanket. Use a packing gauge to check the height of the blanket.

   Remedy:
   Increase packing as required.

Cause B: Increased impression because blanket has become swollen or embossed. This may be due to (1) a blanket with insufficient solvent or oil resistance, (2) continued use of a blanket wash that evaporates too slowly and/or has too high a KB number, or (3) use of ultraviolet (UV) inks.

Remedy 1:
Check the height of the blanket surface with a packing gauge. If the height has increased, remove the indicated thickness of packing.

Remedy 2:
Obtain blankets with better solvent and oil resistance, designed for use with heatset inks.

Remedy 3:
Use a blanket wash that evaporates faster and has a lower KB number. Consult your blanket supplier for recommendations.

Cause C: Use of an incompatible ink-blanket combination. This can cause embossing and excessive pressure in the image areas.

Remedy:
Change to a blanket designed for the ink being used.

Cause D: The blanket surface has lost ink receptiveness by becoming glazed and hard. Such glazing may result from surface oxidation or to accumulation of gum, paper coating, dried ink, or dried varnish.

Remedy:
Sponge the blanket with water with every washing. If blanket becomes glazed, scrub with pumice powder and solvent until the glaze is removed. There are also commercial glaze removers available.

Trouble: **Ghost image** from a previous job appears in solids.

Cause A: The blanket is embossed as a result of ink vehicle absorption during printing of the previous job.

Remedy:
Install a new blanket.

NOTE: Clean the old blanket thoroughly with blanket wash and hang the blanket in a dark area to rest. Absorbed oil will be diffused through the rubber, and the embossing may be reduced.

Cause B: The blanket is debossed due to extraction of soluble materials from the blanket by the ink vehicle.

Remedy:
Install a new blanket. Change to inks that are compatible with the blanket.

Trouble: **Paper tends to stick** to or be picked by the nonprinting areas of the blanket.

Cause: The blanket surface has swollen and become tacky. This is caused by washing the blanket with too strong a solvent or by gum being deposited from fountain solutions that contain alcohol. With the exception of ultraviolet inks, which require special blankets, inks rarely cause synthetic rubber surfaces to become tacky.

Remedy:
Wash the blanket with water and consult blanket supplier for types of compatible washes.

NOTE: Never use sulfur or a sulfur compound on a blanket when printing using copperized aluminum or bimetal plates. Sulfur and sulfides blind the copper image areas.

Trouble: **Impression is uneven** and excessive pressure is required to make all areas print.

Cause A: The blanket is not uniform in thickness. To check this:

1. Remove the plate and packing.

2. Run the press with a thin film of ink on the form rollers, and lower the best form roller only until it contacts the highest parts of the cylinder surfaces. If the plate cylinder proves to be in acceptable shape, take note of the areas of the blanket that have not received a film of ink. These areas are depressed.

Remedy:
Patch the back of the blanket in the low areas with tissues torn to the required shape. Use gum arabic as the adhesive.

NOTE: GATF recommends that all newly received blankets be measured in several areas to determine their uniformity of thickness. Measurements should be made with a device that is recommended for graphic arts use. Each plant should have standards established concerning the acceptable range of thickness in any single blanket. Any blanket not meeting the established thickness standards should be rejected before it goes to the pressroom.

Cause B: One or more warped cylinders.

Remedy 1:
If the dent is not too deep, build it up with tissue torn to the required shape and applied with shellac. Use fine sandpaper on a flat block to taper the edges and smooth down any high spots after the shellac has dried. This procedure is recommended only as a temporary solution.

Remedy 2:
For permanent correction, the cylinder should be built up by metal spraying, or by other means, and then reground.

Trouble: **Blanket surface is smashed** or indented.

Cause: Accidental wrap-up or passage through the press of wadded or crumpled paper, especially heavyweight paper or paperboard.

Remedy 1:
Wash the low area thoroughly with blanket wash to swell it as much as possible. Then put paper patches under the depressed area to bring them up to normal height.

Remedy 2:
Wash the blanket with solvent, soak the fabric backing thoroughly with water, and hang it in a dark place to rest it.

Remedy 3:
Try four-ply or five-ply blankets provided the cylinder undercuts are deep enough. These blankets have somewhat less tendency to smash than three-ply blankets.

Remedy 4:
Use a compressible blanket.

Trouble: **Horizontal streaks** in the printing.

Cause A: A loose and slipping blanket. Because of differences in packing, the surface speeds of the plate and blanket are not always exactly equal. A loose blanket may tend to follow the plate and slip on the blanket cylinder. This slippage is intermittent and causes streaks. The greater the plate-to-blanket pressure, the worse the slippage.

Remedy:
Tighten the blanket. Use the packing gauge to check the plate-to-blanket pressure. If too high, remove the excess packing.

Cause B: Press vibration or bumping due to the presence of the cylinder gaps.

Remedy 1:
Check packing and reduce if indicated.

Remedy 2:
Change to compressible blanket.

8 Paper Troubles

Introduction Papers used in web offset come in a wide variety of types and finishes. Their basis weights (basis: 500 25"x38" sheets) generally range from 20 to 80 pounds (30 to 120 grams per square meter). Heavier weights can be run but do not handle well in folders and must be cut off and delivered in sheets.

Web offset papers have the same general physical and chemical properties as papers for sheetfed presses. They have grain or machine direction, two-sidedness, and hygroscopic properties. They can vary tremendously in quality, depending on the types of fibers used, the fiber preparation, and the surface and finish of the paper.

For satisfactory performance in web offset, papers should meet certain basic requirements. Because they are fed from rolls and printed in web form, some of these requirements differ from those of sheet papers.

Web offset paper requirements
1. **Flatness.** Webs should be flat enough to pass through the printing units without wrinkling or distorting appreciably.

2. **Proper moisture content.** The moisture content of web offset papers is not as critical as that of sheetfed offset papers for the following reasons:

a. In rolls of paper, only the edges parallel to the machine direction or grain are ever exposed to the air. Therefore, the dimensional changes of these edges caused by changes in their moisture content are only one-half to one-fourth as great as those of the across-the-grain edges of sheetfed offset papers.
b. Except for preprinting, roll papers never go through the press more than once, so they are not subject to distortions due to wavy or tight edges that might develop if rolls had to stand between printings.
c. Rolls of paper are usually unwrapped just before printing and are run through the press rapidly. There is little time for the edges of the web to pick up moisture and expand,

Web entering first
printing unit.

or to give off moisture and shrink. This will happen only if
the rolls are improperly protected during transit, storage, or
handling between storage and loading on the press.
d. The paper web is under tension throughout its travel
through the press.
e. Papers for web offset are usually made with a moisture
content of 4.5% to 5.5%. This enables the papermaker to
maintain good uniformity of moisture content and to
minimize wet streaks. In the case of coated papers, this
practice minimizes any tendency to blister in the dryer.

3. **Freedom from dust and lint.** Loose fibers and dust
particles quickly destroy print quality.

4. **Adequate moisture resistance.** The press moisture
should not soften surface sizing or coating adhesive enough
to permit transfer of surface fibers, mineral filler, or coating
pigment to the offset blankets.

5. **Adequate pick resistance.** Surface strength should be
sufficient to prevent picking without excessive reduction of
ink tack.

6. **Freedom from active chemicals.** Paper should contain nothing that tends to sensitize printing plates and cause scumming, or to emulsify the ink and cause tinting.

7. **Good dimensional stability.** In printing, the paper web is under tension all the way from the metering rolls to the cutoff. Uniform mechanical stretch in the across-the-machine direction is necessary for good register.

In addition to these requirements, the condition of the rolls is important. Rolls should be round and tightly wound under proper tension; they should be uniform in diameter from end to end; they should be free from soft spots, welts, corrugations, and water streaks, and they should not be "starred." Rolls should be wrapped at the mill so they are completely protected from the atmosphere to insure that their moisture content is kept uniform throughout.

Roll paper for heatset web offset should be protected by moisture-proof end disks and wrapping materials. These materials protect the paper from the effects of temperature and humidity changes while the paper is in transit and in storage. It must be realized that the paper is in transit within the mill, between mill and printer (sometimes two separate moves), and within the printing plant. Throughout these transit phases, the roll must be so handled that the wrappers are not torn. When rolls are received by the printer, they should be examined, and rolls with damaged wrappers should be set aside and reported to the paper supplier immediately. Company policy and production demands dictate whether or not such rolls are automatically rejected. If the wrapper on a roll is damaged within the plant, it should be repaired immediately.

Paper performance. Core cards for reporting roll performance should be filled out and returned to the mill. This is most important; the mill needs reports of good performance as well as poor performance. In the case of poor performance, even slight problems should be reported, giving the mill as many details as possible. Include samples showing the nature of the problems, if these can be made available. Such detailed and continuous reporting makes it possible for the mills to provide rolls with improved runnability and printability. In some plants, the core cards are the source of information for the plant's own paper performance records.

Paper storage and handling. Although this is a book on troubles, a word concerning waste is justified. In many plants today, great emphasis is placed on running rolls of paper very close to the core before splicing. Claims are made that it is possible to leave 0.125" (3.18 mm) or less on the average core. There is nothing wrong with this approach to saving paper, but it is often true in these same plants that 0.125" or more of paper is routinely slabbed off the outside of the roll when it is being prepared for splicing. In the interest of reducing waste, emphasis should be placed where it really counts. The figure shows the relative value of saving paper on the outside of the roll as compared to what is left on the core. For example, if the outer 0.125" of paper from a 40" (1.0-meter) diameter roll is rewound onto an empty 3.5" (90-mm) core it will make a butt roll that is 5.7" (145 mm) in diameter. The same 0.125" taken from a 50" (1.3-meter) roll will produce a butt roll that is more than 6" (150 mm) in diameter.

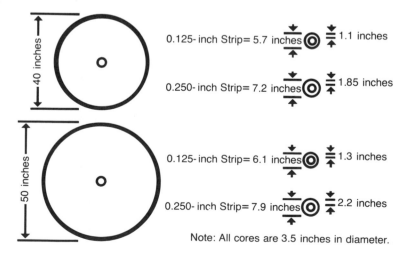

Relative amount of paper that is wasted when paper is stripped off the outside of the paper roll.

40 inches

0.125- inch Strip= 5.7 inches   1.1 inches

0.250- inch Strip= 7.2 inches   1.85 inches

50 inches

0.125- inch Strip= 6.1 inches   1.3 inches

0.250- inch Strip= 7.9 inches   2.2 inches

Note: All cores are 3.5 inches in diameter.

There should be a heavy emphasis placed on reducing damage and unnecessary slabbing off of the outside of rolls from the time they leave the delivery vehicle to the time they are mounted on the press.

This section on "Paper Troubles" is intended to give the web offset pressman a ready reference that will help him (1) avoid paper problems, (2) quickly and correctly diagnose a trouble when it occurs, and (3) apply the proper remedy. Some of the remedies may not be possible under existing operating conditions — the press may not have the equipment or devices mentioned in the suggested remedy; it may not be possible to change the paper at that time; and doctoring heatset inks is not a simple thing to do. For a chronic paper trouble that can only be overcome with equipment or devices not available on the press, the suggested remedy may serve as a guide to management in its investigations of new equipment. Where a remedy suggests changing paper or paper specifications, it is assumed that the paper supplier will be called in as soon as the trouble is identified as a paper problem; and correspondingly the ink supplier when ink is concerned.

The following is a list of the principal paper troubles, with their causes and remedies:

Trouble: **Dented roll.**

Cause: Careless handling or accident. Dents or cuts on ends of roll initiate web breaks.

Remedy 1:
If dent is not deep, sand or cut it out until edges of the paper are smooth.

Remedy 2:
If the dent is deep, print down to the dent, stop the press, slab off the dented area, re-splice, and resume printing. Badly damaged rolls should be returned to the mill.

Trouble: **Out-of-round roll** causes varying tension at the infeed, resulting in misregister.

Cause A: Storing rolls on sides.

Remedy 1:
Store rolls on ends to prevent "flats."

Remedy 2:
Equip press with constant-tension infeed.

Cause B: Too much pressure applied by the lift truck to a loosely wound roll.

Remedy 1:
Reduce the clamp pressure in lifting rolls. Lift trucks that apply vacuum to rolls can use a minimal clamp pressure.

Remedy 2:
Equip press with constant-tension infeed.

Trouble: **Roll is starred** or wavy near core causing tension to vary when feeding from the starred area.

Starred roll of paper. Photo © 1978 TAPPI. Reprinted from Technical Information Sheets, TIS 016-15, with permission.

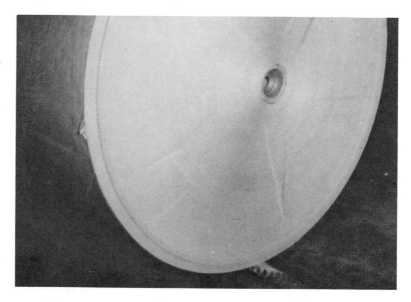

Cause: Increasing tension as roll is wound at the mill.

Remedy:
None, as this is a mill problem. Notify supplier or reject roll, with core card filled out and attached to roll.

Trouble: **Roll is telescoped.**

A roll that has telescoped.
Courtesy of Consolidated Papers, Inc.

Cause: Roll was wound with too little tension.

Remedy:
Return the roll to mill to be rewound; fill out core card and attach to roll.

Trouble: **Roll is corrugated.** Corrugation causes weaving of the web and misregister in printing.

Corrugated roll.
*Courtesy of Consolidated
Papers, Inc.*

Cause A: Moisture content or paper caliper is not uniform across the web.

Remedy 1:
Use a spirally taped roller to spread and flatten the web.

Remedy 2:
Increase the distance (the path) between the roll and the first printing unit to allow the web to flatten out.

Remedy 3:
Equip the press with a constant-tension infeed.

Remedy 4:
Equip the press with a Mount Hope or similar curved roller on the infeed to spread and flatten the web.

Action of a Mt. Hope
curved roller in
spreading or narrowing
the paper web.
*Courtesy of Mt. Hope
Machinery Co.*

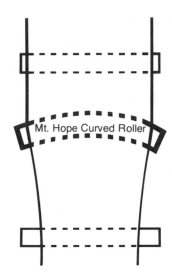

Cause B: Unwrapping rolls in a high humidity area and allowing them to stand for any length of time. Such welts are rarely more than 0.25 inch (6.4 millimeters) deep.

Remedy 1:
Slab off the outer 0.25 inch (6.4 millimeters) of paper.

Remedy 2:
Do not unwrap rolls until just before going to press.

Trouble: **Web wrinkles** or creases in printing. Web is forced to contract, resulting in one or more wrinkles that run lengthwise of the web.

Cause: Web has slack edges due to moisture pickup while in the roll.

Remedy 1:
Prevention. Keep rolls protected from atmospheric changes by leaving wrappers on them until they are mounted on the infeed stand.

Remedy 2:
Adjust the eccentric-mounted infeed roller to balance edge tension.

Remedy 3:
Build up the ends of an infeed roller with tape or paper just under the slack area(s). This helps to flatten the web.

Remedy 4:
Increase the web tension. Stretching the web tends to tighten slack edges.

Remedy 5:
Equip the press with a Mount Hope or similar curved roller on the infeed to spread and flatten the web.

Trouble: **Webs pull tight** or wrinkle on one side although loose on the opposite side after each flying splice. The next roll reverses tension, tight side becomes loose, loose side becomes tight.

Cause: Rolls come from different positions in the paper machine web and have different side-to-side characteristics.

Remedy:
Run rolls in groups according to their position in the papermaking machine. Paper manufacturers will cooperate by color-coding rolls to identify their machine position.

Trouble: **Web breaks** are a serious problem in web offset. They can occur anywhere on the press from the infeed to the cutoff. Breaks result in lost time, paper waste, and often damage to blankets and plates. Excessive tension, if uniform, is not likely to cause web breaks. Most papers have a tensile strength greater than 12 pounds per inch (214 grams per millimeter) of width which would equal 432 pounds (196 kilograms) for a 36-inch (914-millimeter) web.

Cause A: Excessive tension on one or both edges of the web due to loss of moisture and shrinkage, making the web tight-edged and baggy. This condition can start a tear at one edge and cause a web break.

Remedy:
Prevention. Keep rolls completely wrapped until ready to mount on roll stand. If the rolls are stored, make sure wrappings are undamaged.

Cause B: Roll has dent or cut in end. Such defects can start tears that result in web breaks on the press.

Remedy 1:
If dent is not deep, sand or cut it out until edges of the paper are smooth.

Remedy 2:
If the dent is deep, print down to the dent, stop the press, slab off the damaged portion of roll, resplice, and resume printing. Badly damaged rolls should be returned to the supplier with core card filled out and attached.

Cause C: Fiber cuts, hair cuts, wire holes, wrinkles, slime spots, foam spots, calender cuts. Any one of these can start a tear.

Common web defects.
*Courtesy of
Kimberly-Clark Corp.*

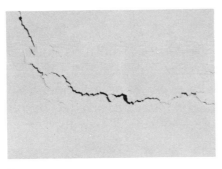

Burst

Hair Cut

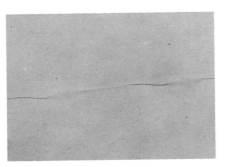

Hard Wrinkle

Calender Cuts

Remedy:
None. If these defects are numerous, call in the supplier.

Cause D: Bad mill splices. Web breaks can occur if the draw across the splice is uneven.

Remedy:
If these troubles are extensive, the problem should be taken up with the mill.

Cause E: Printing units or other press elements may be out of line. This is indicated if a proportionately large number of web breaks occur in one section of the press. An indication of misalignment of press elements is the presence of diagonal wrinkles in any span of web in the press.

Remedy:
Have the press alignment checked, and corrected if necessary.

Trouble: **White, fiber-shaped spots** in solids; and halftones are grainy.

Cause A: Uncoated paper with loosely bonded surface fibers variously referred to as lint, fuzz, fluff, and whiskers. These fibers are lifted by tacky inks even when printing a single color. Once fibers become attached to the blanket or plate, the fibers absorb moisture and refuse to transfer ink.

Remedy 1:
Reduce the tack of the ink as much as possible without affecting print quality.

Remedy 2:
Install a leather-covered or grained rubber form roller, usually in the first-down position. These rollers help to dislodge lint and dust that tend to accumulate on the plates.

Remedy 3:
Discard paper that lints too badly. Fill out core card and attach to the roll.

Cause B: Surface-sized paper in which the surface fibers are not well bonded by hydration, but, to a large extent, are held down by the starch surface size. Such papers usually cause no trouble on a single-color press. But on a multicolor press, moisture from the first unit softens the surface size so that fibers are lifted by the second-down or a later ink.

Remedy 1:
Reduce the plate dampening to a minimum.

Remedy 2:
Try adding one part isopropyl alcohol to three parts dampening solution. This may reduce the dampening solution's softening effect on the starch surface size.

Cause C: Cotton fibers coming from molleton or other fabric dampening roller covers. These are generally easy to distinguish from paper fibers; usually they are fewer in number, and their average length is more than 0.125 inch (3.2 millimeters). Paper fibers are usually shorter.

Remedy 1:
Put new covers on the dampeners.

Remedy 2:
Use parchment paper dampener covers. These covers are replaced very easily and do not shed fibers. They require special base rollers.

Remedy 3:
Consider running bareback or converting to a system that does not require roller covers.

NOTE: Remedies 2 and 3 may cause surging — variations in the amount of dampening solution available to the plate.

Cause D: Brush-type sheet cleaner may be abrading the paper surface and loosening surface fibers.

Remedy 1:
Set sheet cleaner brushes with lighter pressure on the web.

Remedy 2:
Change to a gas flame preheater that can burn lint and fuzz off the web.

Trouble: **Solids on uncoated paper** look and feel rough.

Cause: The surface fibers are not well bonded and are raised, but not actually picked up, by the pull of the ink. This problem can occur when printing a single color or on the second or later unit in multicolor presswork.

Remedy 1:
Reduce the tack of the ink as much as possible without affecting print quality.

Remedy 2:
Install a leather-covered or grained rubber form roller, usually in the first-down position. These rollers help to dislodge lint and dust that tend to accumulate on the plates.

Remedy 3:
Discard paper that lints too badly. Fill out core card and attach to the roll.

Trouble: **Non-fiber-shaped white spots** in solids. The spots repeat on consecutive sheets and increase in number during the run.

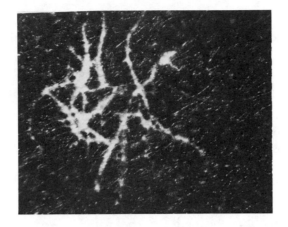

Enlargement of a typical spot caused by paper dust.

Cause A: Loose paper dust on the web. This can be slitter dust, cutter dust, or dryer scale.

Remedy:
Install a vacuum sheet cleaner. Such cleaners are reported to remove much dust, but are not 100% effective. They can cause trouble if set too tight or if brush becomes worn or stiff.

Cause B: Flakes of coating or particles larger than single fibers picked from the paper surface. To distinguish them from loose dust particles, examine the previously printed signatures or sheets until you find the one on which a typical spot first appeared. If examination with a magnifier shows that the paper surface in the original spot was ruptured, the paper was picked. If not, the spot was caused by a loose dust particle.

Paper split in printed solid due to paper weakness or excessive ink tack.

Remedy:
Reduce the ink's tack as much as possible without affecting print quality. If this does not help, the paper may be unsuitable for offset. Consult with both the paper supplier and the ink manufacturer.

NOTE: The use of a leather-covered or grained rubber roller helps to remove and store particles which have adhered to the plate.

Trouble: **Paper picks or splits.** *Picking* refers to rupturing of the paper surface by the pull of the ink in areas larger than single fibers. In *splitting*, large areas of the paper are peeled off and stick to the blanket. Splitting usually causes a web break. Picking and splitting almost always occur or start in solids, seldom in halftone areas.

Cause A: The internal bond strength of the paper is too low or the bonding of coating to the base stock is too weak to withstand the pull of the ink. Have the paper tested. If pick resistance is normal, see Cause B. If pick resistance is weak, try the following remedies:

Remedy 1:
Reduce the ink's tack with a suitable reducer or solvent, or by increasing the dampening water flow.

Remedy 2:
Change to a more pick-resistant paper.

Remedy 3:
Add isopropyl alcohol to the fountain solution to make a 25% alcohol solution.

Remedy 4:
Try reducing the press speed if none of the above remedies solves the problem.

Cause B: The paper has good pick resistance when dry but is weakened by successive applications of moisture in multicolor presswork. In this case, the first-down color prints OK, but the second-, third-, or fourth-down color picks the paper.

Remedy 1:
Reduce the plate moisture and the printing pressure to a minimum.

Remedy 2:
Change to a more moisture-resistant paper.

Trouble: **Paper delaminates.** Delamination is a single-sided, ragged-edge, long-in-the-press-direction problem. Heat blisters, on the other hand, are round or oval defects with well-defined edges and appear on both sides of the web.

Cause: Sharp flexing of the web as it emerges from the impression caused by the web adhering to both blankets simultaneously. When printing solids or heavy halftones on both sides of the web on blanket-to-blanket presses, the web tends to wrap, first on one blanket and then the other. It can start to wrap on one blanket while still adhering to the other, thus causing rapid and sharp flexing. This strongly stresses the fiber bonds within the web and can cause delamination.

Remedy 1:
Reduce the tack of the ink somewhat by increasing the dampening water or by adding solvents to the ink.

Remedy 2:
Reduce the press speed.

Remedy 3:
Run the wire side of the web to the heaviest form.

NOTE: For blistering that occurs in the heat dryer, see Section 10, "Dryer and Chill Stand Troubles."

Trouble: **Paper coating piles** or builds on blankets in nonprinting areas. A little piling does not usually affect print quality, but coating can continue to accumulate until halftones become sandy and highlight dots are lost.

Cause: Running coated or film-coated paper in which the coating adhesive is too moisture-sensitive. Web offset presses will print some coated papers that cannot be run satisfactorily on sheetfed presses because of piling. The reasons for this difference are probably that web printing requires less dampening moisture and is done at higher linear speeds. However, the only foolproof test to distinguish which papers will run and which will not is an actual press run.

Remedy 1:
Avoid coated papers that have poor wet rub resistance unless press tests have shown that they will run. See GATF publication, *What the Printer Should Know about Paper.*

Remedy 2:
Add one part isopropyl alcohol to three parts dampening solution. This reduces the solubility of starch coating adhesives.

Trouble: **Uncoated paper piles on blankets.**

Cause: Fibers and filler being pulled from the paper are accumulating on the blanket.

Remedy 1:
Reduce tack of ink.

Remedy 2:
Increase blanket packing by 0.002" (0.05 mm). Increased pressure will help scrub accumulated material off the blanket.

Remedy 3:
Run more water to lubricate blanket.

Remedy 4:
If using compressible blankets, change to conventional.

Trouble:

Paper coating piles in the middle halftone printing areas of blankets. After one to two thousand impressions, the middle halftones develop a mottled appearance due to dot slur, and the blanket shows a lumpy buildup in those areas. This never happens on the first unit but only on later units of multicolor presses.

Effect on print of piling on blanket.

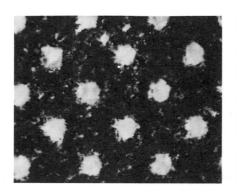
Slight Piling

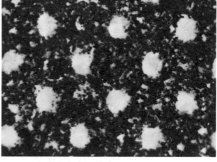
Moderate Piling

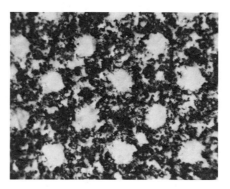
Severe Piling

Cause:

The coating adhesive is being softened and rendered tacky by moisture on the first unit, so a following unit can lift adhesive and coating pigment. The removed adhesive and pigment mix with the ink, producing a puttylike combination that sticks to the blanket and gradually produces a buildup of appreciable thickness. Frequent blanket wash-ups with water and ink solvent are needed to remove the piling. Strangely enough, papers that cause this trouble generally show good wet rub resistance.

Remedy 1:
Change to a better paper. Unfortunately, there is no reliable test for papers that cause this trouble.

Remedy 2:
Try adding one part isopropyl alcohol to three parts dampening solution.

Trouble: **Overall tint** quickly appears on the unprinted areas of coated paper. This tint may appear on the non-image areas of the plates but can be washed off with water sponge. If another paper is substituted, the tint disappears but quickly returns on going back to the original paper.

Cause: The fountain solution is extracting a surface-active agent from the paper coating, causing the ink to emulsify in the plate moisture.

Remedy 1:
Stiffen the ink as much as possible with a suitable varnish (consult inkmaker), or try another stiffer ink.

Remedy 2:
Change fountain solution, increase fountain solution pH.

Remedy 3:
Avoid the use of any wetting agent in the fountain solution.

Remedy 4:
Get another paper.

Trouble: **Paper yellows** on passing through the dryer.

Cause: The paper web has been overheated. Some papers discolor more than others at the same temperature.

Remedy 1:
Reduce the heat in the dryer.

Remedy 2:
Speed up the press.

9 Ink Troubles

Introduction   Basically, lithographic ink is a dispersion of a pigment in a fluid vehicle that will print and dry. The pigment provides the color and determines whether the printed ink film will be transparent or opaque. The vehicle gives the ink fluidity so that it can be distributed by the press inking rollers and applied evenly to the paper. In the printed ink film, the liquid vehicle must be changed to a solid in order to bind the pigment to the printed surface.

The various types of lithographic inks differ primarily in their method of drying. In sheetfed lithography, inks may be divided into two classes: inks whose vehicle is principally drying oil and that dry by a combination of absorption and chemical action, namely, oxidation and polymerization; and inks, generally referred to as "quickset," whose vehicle is composed of drying oils, resins, and solvents that speed up setting by a process of selective absorption and that dry by oxidation and polymerization. Inks of these two classes are also used in web offset printing on uncoated papers and newsprint where use of a heat dryer is unnecessary. Heatset inks are those which are dried by evaporation of their solvents with the aid of heat, followed by chilling to solidify the remaining nonvolatile resins in their vehicle. Heatset inks are not dry in the sense of being setoff-free when the web has passed through the dryer. At this point, the ink film on the paper web is in a semifluid state because of its high temperature. Passing the web over a chilling unit results in **setting** the ink sufficiently to make possible finishing operations without smearing, smudging, or setoff. Actually, the ink may still retain a little solvent, which gradually evaporates later on. Final hardening may be the result of long-term oxidation.

The vehicle in heatset inks is principally resins dissolved in a volatile solvent that boils between 350-550°F (177-388°C). The inks are designed for web operations where the printed web is passed through a heater (commonly referred to as a dryer) and then over chilling rollers. The function of the dryer is to raise the temperature of the printed web to a point where the volatile solvents are evaporated, leaving the resin in the ink to bind the pigment to the paper. On common-impression-cylinder presses, the web is passed through the dryer after printing one side, and again after the second side is printed. On blanket-to-blanket presses, the web passes throught the dryer only once. Heatset inks may be slightly modified by adding drying oils and drier to increase their rub- and scuff-resistance. If too much of such materials are added, they may cause the inks to remain tacky after passing over the chill rolls.

Basically, lithographic inks differ from other printing inks in that they must work with water. Dampening water always mixes to some extent with the ink during printing, but the ink must not waterlog and become pasty. Also, the ink should not break down and mix with the water; otherwise, a tint of the ink would be printed where the paper should be blank. The inkmaker selects the proper pigments and vehicles and adjusts the ink's body to meet these requirements.

Another way in which offset inks differ markedly from the inks for other printing processes is in the amount of ink that is applied to the paper. The table lists the measured thickness of dried ink films for various printing processes. The ink film thickness for offset lithography is much thinner and therefore the ink must be more pigmented. High pigmentation is one of the factors that make offset inks more difficult to manufacture and use.

Offset lithography	0.00008"	(0.002 mm)
Letterpress	0.00020"	(0.005 mm)
Gravure	0.00050"	(0.013 mm)
Screen (thin film)	0.00125"	(0.032 mm)
Screen (thick film)	0.00250"	(0.064 mm)

Because of the many variables in both inkmaking and lithography, the web offset pressman is constantly faced with situations that require knowledge, experience, and good judgment. Some knowledge can be gained through study; and, for this purpose, GATF has published *What the Printer Should Know about Ink.*

Experience and judgment come with practice. The inkmaker, of course, is a key person when ink problems arise. In most cases it is not practical to "doctor" inks in a web offset operation because of the difficulty of maintaining uniformity of the doctoring throughout a run. It is also dangerous to doctor an ink on the press without the inkmaker's advice and instructions because of the complexity of the heatset ink formulas. A typical heatset ink may contain 15 to 30 different ingredients. When making the ink, these materials must be added in a prescribed sequence; quite often, groups of raw materials must be mixed separately. This is why the inkmaker must be consulted before any effort is made to solve a problem by doctoring the ink.

The importance of good communications between the printer and inkmaker cannot be overestimated. When inks are ordered, the inkmaker can make use of the following information:

1. Speed of press
2. Type and length of dryer
3. Chill capacity
4. Type of paper
5. Take-off rate
6. End use of product

This section on "Ink Troubles" is intended to give the web offset pressman a ready reference that will help him (1) avoid ink troubles; (2) diagnose a problem quickly and correctly when it arises; and (3) apply the proper remedy.

Some of the remedies may not be possible under existing operating conditions — the press may not have the equipment or devices mentioned in a suggested remedy; it may not be possible to change the paper at the time; doctoring heatset inks should be avoided. For chronic ink problems that can only be overcome with equipment or devices not available on the press, the suggested remedy may serve as a guide to management in its investigation of new equipment. Where a remedy suggests changing paper or paper specifications, it is assumed that the paper supplier will be called in as soon as the trouble is identified as a paper problem; and correspondingly, the ink supplier when ink is concerned.

Following are some troubles that originate with ink:

Trouble: **Ink marks in delivery.**

See first-listed trouble, "Ink fails to dry, marks on chill rolls, and smears in delivery," in Section 10, "Dryer and Chill Stand Troubles."

Trouble: **Setoff** of heatset ink in folding and finishing operations.

Cause A: Dryer temperature is too low for the speed of the web, and the ink solvent is not being completely evaporated.

Remedy:
Either raise the temperature in the dryer or reduce the speed of the press. Consult your inkmaker about the use of a more volatile heatset solvent.

Cause B: Ink contains too much drying oil in proportion to resin and remains tacky when dry.

Remedy 1:
Increase the dryer temperature.

Remedy 2:
Reduce the press speed.

Remedy 3:
Have the ink reformulated.

Remedy 4:
Change to a more suitable ink.

Cause C: Chill system is not adequate. The ink resins are not setting hard enough.

Remedy 1:
Lower the chill water temperature. Web temperature on leaving the chill rolls should be no higher than 90°F (32°C) — this is cool to the touch.

Remedy 2:
Reduce the press speed and the dryer temperature.

Remedy 3:
Check the water temperature in the rolls. Increase its flow if the outlet temperature is too high.

Remedy 4:
Increase the wrap of the web around the chill rolls or install additional chill rolls.

Cause D: Inadequate scavenging of vapors that cling to the web as it leaves the dryer.

Remedy 1:
Increase velocity of air in air-knife scavenger at dryer exit.

Remedy 2:
If there is no air-knife scavenger, one should be installed.

Cause E: Ink film thickness is excessive.

Remedy:
Run less ink. If necessary, use an ink with more color strength.

Trouble: **Heatset ink fails to dry** rub-resistant. When heatset ink does not dry hard enough in the dryer and chill-roll section, the result is setoff and smudging in folding and binding operations. However, there is sometimes further drying by oxidation and polymerization that increases the rub- and scuff-resistance of the heat-dried ink.

Cause A: Solvent boils at too high a temperature, or there is insufficient drying oil or drier in the ink.

Remedy:
Consult inkmaker regarding reformulation of the ink to give better rub- and scuff-resistance.

Cause B: Too much acid in the dampening water. Acid can retard or prevent drying of inks that contain drying oil and drier.

Remedy:
Prevention. Keep the fountain solution pH above 4.5 and preferably between 5.0 and 6.0.

A pH Meter.
Courtesy of Analytical Measurements, Inc.

Trouble: **Printed ink chalks.** Chalking occurs when the printed and dried ink can be rubbed off, leaving the paper more or less clean. In other words, the ink is not well bonded to the paper. This condition is sometimes called "fried ink."

Cause: Too high a temperature in the dryer, causing excessive absorption of ink vehicle by the paper and leaving the pigment with insufficient binder.

Remedy:
Reduce the gas flame impingement on the web and increase the hot air circulation if possible. Avoid excessive web temperature.

Trouble: **Ink picks, splits, or tears the paper.** This can be an ink trouble, a paper trouble, or both. Either the ink is excessively tacky, or the paper has too little pick resistance for printing with an ink having normal tack for the press size and desired speed. Since picking, splitting, and blistering troubles are often caused by paper weaknesses, they are also discussed in Section 8, "Printing Unit Troubles: Paper Picks or Splits," and Section 3, "Printing Unit Troubles: Overheating."

Cause A: The ink is too tacky for the paper.

Remedy 1:
Reduce the tack with a suitable solvent (consult with inkmaker).

Remedy 2:
Increase dampening solution feed to reduce the ink tack.

Remedy 3:
Avoid running ink spare. Thin ink films require more force to split. Check with the inkmaker regarding the possibility of getting an ink with less pigment content so that a heavier ink film can be run.

Remedy 4:
Change to a more pick-resistant paper.

Cause B: Heatset inks lose some solvent by evaporation and become more tacky during the press run. Evaporation is aggravated by heating of the inking system during a run. See Section 3, "Printing Unit Troubles: Overheating."

Remedy 1:
Add the proper solvent to the ink (consult inkmaker).

Remedy 2:
Cool the ink vibrators by circulating water through them to prevent heating up the ink and the consequential evaporation of ink solvent. Or chill the fountain solution by

refrigeration. Refer to the discussion of chilled inkers in the introduction to "Printing Unit Troubles."

Remedy 3:
Thin ink films require more energy to split. Therefore, reduce the ink's color strength and run more of it. This remedy is often overlooked.

Remedy 4:
Ink fed to a light form requires a longer time to work through the inking system than it would if fed to a heavy form. In this case, use a solvent with a somewhat higher boiling point.

Remedy 5:
Chill the fountain solution by refrigeration or even by adding ice cubes to the fountain. Either method is at best a stopgap solution.

Cause C: When a press is being started up, intermittent stops allow time for a loss of ink solvent by evaporation, resulting in increased tack.

Remedy 1:
When making ready for the press run, use "start-up" inks which contain little or no volatile solvents for register and color. Consult inkmaker.

Remedy 2:
Soften the press ink at the start to counteract the stiffening due to loss of solvent during makeready. Once the run is started and the ink flow established, the regular ink may cause no trouble.

Remedy 3:
Spray the ink rollers with a little heatset oil to keep the ink from drying.

Trouble: **Ink backs away** from the fountain roller.

Cause: The ink sets up in the fountain, and it fails to flow and replace the ink that is removed by the fountain roller.

Remedy 1:
Work the ink in the fountain frequently to keep it flowing properly.

Remedy 2:
Install an ink fountain agitator. Generally, inks which do not require an ink fountain agitator do not have enough "body" to print sharply. This is especially true when printing on coated papers.

Trouble: **Ink piles** or cakes on the rollers, plate, or blanket.

Cause A: Ink piles and dries on the ends of the rollers and blanket outside the web area because it has no place to go.

Remedy:
Run with less ink.

Cause B: Ink piles on the printing areas of the plate and blanket because ink is too short, waterlogged, poorly ground, or contains a coarse, heavy pigment.

Remedy 1:
Reduce the dampening to a minimum.

Remedy 2:
Consult the inkmaker. Have the ink reground or reformulated.

Cause C: Ink piles on the blanket in halftone areas but not in solids when printing on coated stock because coating material is being picked up from the paper, being mixed with the ink, and causing piling.

Remedy 1:
Change to a better paper. Unfortunately, there is no reliable test to determine which papers cause this trouble.

Remedy 2:
Try adding one part isopropyl alcohol to three parts dampening solution.

Cause D: Rollers or blanket are new and have not become saturated with ink vehicle or solvent.

Remedy:
Apply a commercially available compound that will not affect drying, but will decrease ink solvent penetration into the rollers and blanket.

Trouble: **Plate prints a tint** of ink on non-image areas. The tint can be seen on the printed sheets and may or may not be visible on the plate. The tint is not tight to the plate but can be washed off with water. However, it quickly reappears when printing is resumed.

Cause A: The ink is not sufficiently water-resistant and emulsifies in the dampening solution.

Remedy 1:
Add heavy varnish to soft or soupy ink to increase body.

Remedy 2:
Add water-resistant varnish to short, easily waterlogged ink.

Cause B: The non-image areas of the plate have not been sufficiently desensitized because of incomplete removal of a bichromated-colloid plate coating. This cause may apply to both surface and deep-etch plates. To check this, wash all tint off the plate, polish part of a blank area with a scotch stone or snakeslip, and give the entire plate a light etch. If, when the run is resumed, the polished area remains clean while the surrounding area tints, the cause is residual coating. If all areas continue to tint, the cause is either the paper (see Cause C) or breakdown of the ink (see Cause D). If the test indicates the presence of a residual coating, proceed as follows:

Remedy 1:
Send the plate back to the plateroom for further treatment. See plate posttreatment in the GATF publication *Offset Lithographic Platemaking.*

Remedy 2:
In the case of an aluminum deep-etch plate with residual coating, wash the plate with the following solution:

Oxalic acid .....6 ounces (0.18 liter)
Hot water........8 ounces (0.24 liter)

Apply with a rag or sponge, then wash off with water and proceed to print.

Cause C: An emulsifying or sensitizing agent is being extracted from the paper coating. This is a likely possibility if the substitution of another paper stops the tinting.

Remedy 1:
Stiffen the ink as much as possible or try another ink. Consult with your inkmaker.

Remedy 2:
Avoid use of a wetting agent in the fountain solution.

Remedy 3:
Use another paper.

Cause D: The ink is not sufficiently water-resistant and is broken down by the plate moisture. In single-color presswork, if changing the paper does not stop the tinting, the trouble is either with the ink or the plate. In multicolor presswork, if all the inks are tinting, the cause is most likely the paper (see Cause C). If one or two inks are tinting while the others are printing clean, ink or plate trouble is indicated.

Remedy:
Consult the inkmaker with regard to stiffening the ink or replacing the ink.

NOTE: Inks designed for large or high-speed presses are likely to break down and tint when run on small presses at low speed because of the low tack of the ink.

Trouble:

Ink causes printing plate to scum. Such scum is usually visible on the plate and cannot be removed with a wet sponge. If the scum is very light, it can be removed by re-etching the plate.

Cause A:

Halftones are being printed with too much ink or with an ink that is too soft. The ink squashes and spreads over the nonprinting areas between the dots, gradually sensitizing them.

Remedy:
Run the ink on halftones as stiff and spare as possible.

Cause B:

Abrasive pigment particles or aggregates in the ink. These gradually wear the plate at the margins of its image areas, causing dots and lines to thicken. Presence of pigment particles or aggregates may be determined with the Fineness-of-Grind Gauge or Grindometer (see GATF publication *What the Printer Should Know about Ink*).

Remedy 1:
Have the ink reground.

Remedy 2:
Replace it with a better ink.

NOTE: Other causes of plate sensitization and scumming are discussed in "Ink Feed Troubles: Roller and Blanket Streaks" and "Plate Troubles: Non-Image Areas Become Greasy."

Trouble:

Ink fails to trap properly on preceding colors. Most multicolor web offset printing involves wet trapping of inks, or the ability to print ink films over wet ink films to produce intermediate colors. Whether the desired colors are produced or not depends (1) on the relative amounts of the ink films supplied and (2) on the amounts of available inks actually transferred. Obviously, for proper color reproduction, proper adjustment of the successive ink feeds is of prime importance.

Photomicrograph showing poor wet-trapping of cyan on yellow.

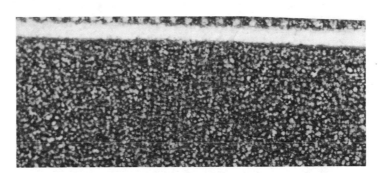

Theoretically, in order to trap or transfer properly, each successive ink should be lower in tack than the preceding ink. Practically, this rule applies mainly to printing on nonabsorbent surfaces such as laminated foils and plastics. On absorbent papers, ink films can increase considerably in tack between printing units by "setting," so that tacks of the successive inks may not be too important. An important factor is the relative strengths of the successive inks. If the first-down ink is strong and must be run spare, the second-down ink may trap even though it is tackier. On the other hand, if the second-down ink is strong and must be run spare, it may not trap on the first-down ink if the first-down ink was run full. However, if a third color is superimposed on the first two, the ink must generally be less tacky than the second-down ink. Setting of the second-down ink, with resultant increase in its tack, is greatly retarded by the first-down ink, even on absorbent stock. As a result, knowledge of ink tacks, color strengths, and the ink-absorbency qualities of paper, and good judgment in press operation are important in avoiding trapping troubles.

A way in which good trapping can be accomplished is to use inks which contain gelled varnishes. The addition of a gellant makes an ink more thixotropic. This means that the ink tends to become very stiff if it is not being worked; such inks require ink fountain agitators. However, the inks flow through the inking system readily because they are being worked by the action of the rollers, the plate, and the blanket. Once these inks are printed, they set up rather quickly and make a good base for subsequent inks. The quick setting reduces the tendency to back-trap on subsequent blankets and decreases the tendency for individual dots to be changed by the pressures of following nips. Such inks print more sharply, giving greater fidelity in both highlight and shadow areas. One drawback to gelled inks is that, due to the action of the gellant, they are quite stiff in the can and require extra effort for loading into the fountain.

The accuracy of colors produced by wet-trapping of solids on solids is affected by changes in gloss. What the eye sees is the combined effect of trapping and gloss, or apparent trapping, which is best measured with a reflection densitometer. Determination of trapping performance is best accomplished by printing control patches of the color inks by themselves and as overlaps of these inks in pairs. The GATF Color Strip is designed for this purpose. From densitometer measurements of the patches, it is possible to calculate and control the degree of trapping.

For a more detailed discussion of ink trapping and its measurement and control, see the topic "Trapping" in the GATF publication *Color Separation Photography*.

The above discussion applies mainly to the trapping of solids on solids. When halftones are superimposed on solids or halftones, another factor, dot spread, can affect the resultant color. Some dot spread is unavoidable in production printing; the problem is to control dot spread by making allowances in the plates by controlling prepress operations. The GATF Dot Gain Scale makes such control possible (see Research Progress Report No. 69).

Control of dot spread in printing depends mainly on not running too much ink, on proper setting of form rollers, and on proper cylinder pressures, both plate-to-blanket and blanket-to-paper. Pressmen sometimes blame poor multicolor tints and halftone colors on poor trappings of inks, but presswork is at fault if solids are trapping properly as indicated by the solid overlaps on the GATF Color Test Strip. (See GATF publication, *What the Printer Should Know about Ink*.)

Failure of inks to trap properly is usually due to one of the following causes:

Cause A: Too much tack in relation to the preceding ink.

Remedy 1:
Reduce the tack of the ink that fails to trap properly.

Remedy 2:
Reduce the color strength of the ink that fails to trap properly and run more of it.

Remedy 3:
Use inks with gellants added.

Remedy 4:
Secure inks with successively decreasing tacks for multicolor presswork.

Cause B: Inks improperly balanced as to color strength. This can result in having to run one color full and the following color spare, in which case the color run spare may not trap.

Remedy 1:
Run the spare ink first-down.

Remedy 2:
Reduce the color strength of the ink being run spare, and run more of it.

Cause C: Increase of ink tack due to heating up of ink drums and rollers, causing loss of ink solvent. This is aggravated if the web is preheated at the infeed but not chilled.

Remedy 1:
Having vibrating ink drums water-cooled to prevent heating up and to maintain them at constant temperature. Refer to the discussion of chilled inkers in the introduction to "Printing Unit Troubles."

Remedy 2:
Use a little heatset oil to reduce the tack of overprinting inks that fail to trap. This procedure will reduce the tendency of the units to heat up during printing and compensate for the loss of solvent by evaporation.

Remedy 3:
Increase the feed of the ink that fails to trap properly and reduce its color strength if necessary.

Trouble: **Halftones show poor trapping,** dot spread, and improper color, although trapping in solids is good.

Cause: Poor ink-water balance — too much ink, too much water, or both.

Remedy:
Cut back ink feed until the ink film on the vibrator nearest the dampener is not more than 0.004 inch (0.01 millimeter) thick on areas corresponding to printing areas; then reduce dampening to a minimum.

NOTE: The ink film measurement can be made with a wet-film gauge, such as the IPI Wet-Film Thickness Gauge manufactured by Gardner Laboratories.

Trouble: **Colors change** during the run with no changes in inks or paper.

Cause A: Increasing temperature of the inking systems as the run progresses. This increases the ink tack through the loss of volatile solvents.

Remedy 1:
Have vibrating ink drums water-cooled to maintain a constant ink temperature. Refer to the discussion of chilled inkers in the introduction to "Printing Unit Troubles."

Remedy 2:
Reduce ink tack if at all possible.

Cause B: Day-to-day or seasonal changes in the pressroom temperature.

Remedy 1:
Have vibrating ink drums water-cooled to maintain a constant ink temperature. Refer to the discussion of chilled inkers in the introduction to "Printing Unit Troubles."

Remedy 2:
Run inks with higher tack as pressroom temperature increases.

Trouble: **Printing is mottled.**

Cause A: Uncoated stock has wild formation and nonuniform ink absorbency which can be verified by making a K & N Ink Absorbency Test or a flexible-blade ink-wipe test. (See GATF publications *What the Lithographer Should Know about Ink* and *What the Printer Should Know about Paper*.)

Remedy 1:
Use inks with maximum color strength and minimum penetrating qualities.

Remedy 2:
Get a better grade of paper.

Cause B: Running too much ink on hard stock that is not ink-receptive.

Remedy:
Use ink with greater color strength and run less of it.

Cause C: Excessive printing pressure.

Remedy 1:
Reduce printing pressure.

Remedy 2:
Stiffen the ink.

Cause D: Too much dampening solution. Moisture reduces the ink's tack so that the ink tends to squash. Moisture also causes minute white spots (snowflakiness) in solids.

Remedy:
Run with a minimum of dampening solution.

Trouble: **Ghost images** appear in solids or halftones.

Cause A: A narrow solid ahead of or behind a wider solid is robbing the form rollers of the ink needed to print full-strength color in a corresponding area of the wider solid. The same result is noticeable in darker halftones.

Remedy 1:
Whenever possible, make layout with solids, halftones, and type well distributed.

Remedy 2:
Run a minimum of dampening water.

Remedy 3:
Avoid running colors spare to produce tints. Make the color weaker and run more of it.

Remedy 4:
If possible, use opaque inks rather than transparent inks.

Remedy 5:
Cut down on the movement of the vibrating drums. This enables more ink to be confined to narrow areas of high demand and may in some cases reduce the ghosting.

Cause B: The blanket is embossed as a result of ink-vehicle absorption during printing of the previous job.

Remedy:
Install a new blanket.

NOTE: Clean an embossed blanket thoroughly with a blanket wash and hang it in a dark area to rest. This treatment will allow absorbed oil to diffuse through the rubber and may reduce the embossing.

Trouble: **Hickeys** are usually doughnut-shaped white spots surrounding a small spot of ink. Hickeys are caused by hard particles of dried ink, drier skin, roller composition, dirt, plaster, or other foreign matter in the ink. White spots in solids that are not doughnut-shaped are caused by paper dust or particles picked up from the paper. These spots, often called hickeys, are discussed in Section 8, "Paper Troubles: Non-Fiber-Shaped White Spots."

Enlargement of a typical hickey.

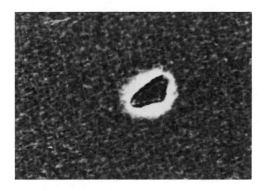

Cause A: Particles of dried ink.

Remedy 1:
Prevention. Avoid dried ink skin when removing ink from cans or kits. Protect ink remaining in a can or kit from oxidation drying and formation of ink skin.

Remedy 2:
Clean the press thoroughly and remove all dried ink in the fountain or on the rollers before inking up the press.

Remedy 3:
Prevent the ink in the ink fountain from mixing with dried ink around the edges of the ink mass.

Remedy 4:
Prevent ink from caking on the ends of rollers by lubrication and manual washing.

Remedy 5:
Use a leather-covered or a grained rubber roller. This will pick up hickeys that are passed on to the plate. Remove the leather-covered rollers and clean them thoroughly at least twice a week. Grained rubber rollers are not as effective as leather-covered rollers, but they require less maintenance.

Cause B: Flakes of roller composition, usually from glazed or pitted rollers.

Remedy 1:
Recondition the form rollers and drums to remove glaze. Glaze is due to accumulations of dried ink vehicle and gum not removed by ordinary wash-up solvents. Use one of the specially formulated glaze-removing materials. Remove the form rollers, and alternately scrub the form rollers and the drums with pumice powder and ink solvent to remove the glaze.

Remedy 2:
Use a leather-covered or a grained rubber roller. This will pick up hickeys that are passed on to the plate. Remove the leather-covered rollers and clean them thoroughly at least twice a week. Grained rubber rollers are not as effective as leather-covered rollers, but they require less maintenance.

Cause C: Particles of dirt, plaster, and other materials have fallen into the press from the ceiling.

Remedy 1:
Vacuum clean the ceiling and everything overhead where dirt can accumulate. Paint the ceiling if necessary, or hang plastic sheeting over the press to catch the falling particles.

Remedy 2:
Use a leather-covered or a grained rubber roller. This will pick up hickeys that are passed on to the plate. Remove the leather-covered rollers and clean them thoroughly at least twice a week. Grained rubber rollers are not as effective as leather-covered rollers, but they require less maintenance.

Trouble: **Ink flies or mists,** forming fine droplets or filaments that become diffused throughout the atmosphere of the pressroom. Ink flying can be either an ink or a press problem.

How an ink splits as it emerges from the roller nip and forms flying particles.

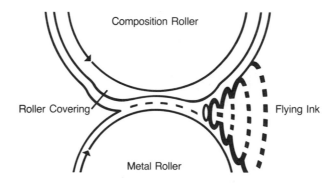

Cause A: Too much ink. The thicker the ink film on the press rollers, the longer the filaments formed when the ink film is split between rollers.

Remedy:
Substitute a more highly pigmented ink and run less of it.

Cause B: The fountain is feeding too thick an ink film to the fountain roller.

Remedy:
Tighten the fountain blade to reduce the ink film thickness and adjust the ratchet to give the roller more movement.

Cause C: The ink is too long and too tacky.

Remedy:
Add a shortening material such as a wax compound, but first consult the inkmaker.

Cause D: Not enough lateral distribution—too little sidewise motion of the vibrating drums allows the ink to form ridges on the rollers and increases its tendency to fly.

Remedy:
Increase the vibration until the ridging disappears.

Trouble: **Printing lacks desired gloss.** One advantage of web offset is its ability to produce glossy printing without the use of antisetoff sprays. Quick evaporation of the solvent by heat and air circulation reduces absorption of ink vehicle by the paper, giving good ink holdout, which is one factor in producing gloss. Other factors are paper smoothness and gloss—the reasons for the bulk of color work being done on coated papers. High gloss is desirable because it enhances the brilliance and intensity of colors. Failure to obtain gloss may be the result of the following causes:

Cause A: The ink vehicle is too fluid and penetrating for the paper.

Remedy 1:
Change to a less absorbent paper.

Remedy 2:
Ink should be reformulated with a less penetrating vehicle. Consult the inkmaker.

NOTE: Ultraviolet (UV) inks have inherently lower gloss because the UV drying system provides little chance for vehicle outflow.

Cause B: The paper is too absorbent.

Remedy 1:
Formulate a suitable ink.

Remedy 2:
Change to a less absorbent paper or a paper with a coating designed to give better ink holdout.

Cause C: Too high a temperature in the dryer makes the resin binder too fluid and penetrating, causing reduced gloss. The result is sometimes called "fried ink."

Remedy 1:
Reduce the dryer temperature and/or increase the press speed.

Remedy 2:
Reformulate the ink with a more volatile solvent to enable the dryer temperature to be reduced.

Cause D: Running with too much dampening water. Excessive moisture in the ink prevents the smooth ink lay necessary for high gloss.

Remedy:
Reduce the dampening water to a minimum.

Trouble: **Ink pigment bleeds.**

Cause A: The ink pigment is dissolving in the heatset ink vehicle and penetrating the paper. Printed color values are thus increased, especially in highlight tints.

Remedy:
Discuss with inkmaker. Ask for pigment that does not bleed. (See GATF publication *What the Printer Should Know about Ink.*)

Cause B: The use of isopropyl alcohol in the fountain water causes some pigments to bleed.

Remedy 1:
Avoid alcohol in the dampening water.

Remedy 2:
Obtain an ink with pigment that does not bleed in alcohol.

Trouble: **Printed halftones show higher values than the plate image shows.**

Cause A: Too much form rollers-to-plate, plate-to-blanket, or blanket-to-blanket pressures.

Remedy:
Check roller settings and packing; set correctly.

Cause B: The ink is too soupy and is squashing in the impression.

Remedy:
Get a stiffer, shorter ink. Consult inkmaker.

Cause C: Halftone dots are slurred or doubled.

Remedy:
For a discussion of doubling and slurring, see "Printing Unit Troubles: Doubling" and "Printing Unit Troubles: Slurring."

Cause D: Plate was not made sharp enough to compensate for normal dot spread on the press.

Remedy:
Have cameraman and platemaker cooperate in making sharper halftone negatives, positives, and plates to allow for press gain. Use of the GATF Dot Gain Scale on plates will enable control of dot sizes in printing (see GATF Research Progress Report No. 69).

10 Dryer and Chill Stand Troubles

Introduction
High-speed multicolor web offset perfecting would not be possible without heatset inks and heat dryers. Heat dryers were in use for heatset letterpress printing in the 1930s, but heatset offset inks were not generally available until the middle 1950s. Since then, inks, papers, and dryers have been going through a process of evolution as a result of research and practical experience.

Paper and ink properties as well as press speeds enter into the design of dryers. (See "Paper Troubles" and "Ink Troubles" for a fuller discussion of paper and heatset ink characteristics.) The paper web must not be heated any more than is absolutely necessary. Excessive heat removes extra moisture, and this moisture loss makes signature handling difficult in postpress operations. The signatures are subject to dimensional changes because of moisture take-up. The dimensional changes can occur in the finished product.

If coated papers are heated up too rapidly, their moisture will be converted into water vapor faster than it can escape. The result is blistering. Basis weight of the paper is also involved. Heavy papers have more total moisture than lightweight papers and require either longer dryers or slower press speeds.

Surface temperature measurements on the web as it leaves the dryer are in the range of 190°-390°F (88°-199°C). At these temperatures, the properties of the paper change due to loss of moisture. The paper becomes brittle and may crack in folding. The paper also shrinks, and this can affect cutoff register. Obviously, a lower drying temperature is better for the paper. Too high a web temperature is the cause of most ink drying problems, including blistering, marking in the folder, loss of gloss, fold cracking, paper discoloration, curl, chalking of ink, and the early aging of printed stock.

The nature of the inks used also affects the dryer design. The more volatile their solvents, the lower the temperature or the shorter time needed to evaporate them. However, fast-drying inks (those with low boiling point solvents) are unstable and tend to dry on the press. The amount of ink being run also determines the time the ink is in the inking system. This affects the amount of evaporation of the solvent and is therefore a factor in the ink formulation.

Dryer design in relation to press speed is one limiting factor when the pressman has an ink drying problem. The capacity of the chill rolls is another. While temperature can be controlled in both dryer and chill roll, the range within which a particular ink-paper combination will work properly is rather limited. Press speed may be varied to produce a change in web temperature, but if press speed is increased, folder problems may result; if press speed is decreased, delivery schedules may not be met. If the ideal solution is a change in dryer design, this can be considered only as a long-range possibility and then only if the problem is chronic. Changing the paper, where this is indicated as the best possible solution, is rarely practical once the job is on the press. Ink, in addition to limited temperature control, is the only item that can be modified with a reasonable degree of speed. But then, quality may be sacrificed.

Satisfactory ink drying, therefore, depends on the **proper balance** of a number of factors: paper, ink, press speed, dryer length, dryer temperature, dryer design, and chill roll capacity. With any given situation, the pressman can only vary the press speed, regulate heat in the dryer, adjust the chill-roll temperature, and, to a slight degree, modify the ink.

The combination of press dryer is usually designed to do a specific job or type of job. The main criteria for success are press speed and the ability to deliver clean sheets or signatures. Much developmental work is being done to increase the efficiency of dryers and to keep dryer length to a minimum. In one system, initial heating of the printed web is accomplished by direct gas-flame impingement that starts evaporation of the ink solvent and burns off some of the released vapors. The heated web is then scrubbed by hot air jets to remove solvent vapors that continue to be evolved, and to continue the solvent's evaporation. Another system uses the recently developed high-velocity air dryers in which only hot air jets or knives heat the web and remove the solvent vapors.

Most high-velocity hot air dryers use designs that allow the web to run very close to the nozzle. With proper design, the air between the nozzle and the web is quite turbulent. This turbulence is used to scrub solvent-laden air off the surface of the web. Most dryers today use a staggered placement in which nozzles are placed alternately above and below the web. Staggered placement forces the web to change direction slightly as it goes through the dryer. The change in direction effectively eliminates the tendency for wrinkles parallel to the running direction to form in the dryer.

Infrared pyrometer used to determine the surface temperature of the web as it exits from the dryer.

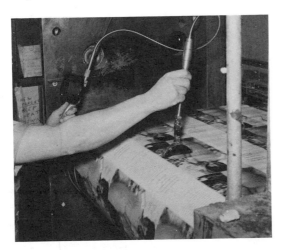

After the web leaves the dryer, ink temperatures are high enough to cause the resins and binders in the ink to become semifluid. The ink must therefore be cooled sufficiently so that it can be delivered without marking; the temperature of the web should be reduced to 90°F (32°C). Cooling is the function of the chill roll section. Chill rolls should be of the "jacketed" type and should be positioned so that maximum linear contact with the web is possible. On existing equipment, the positioning of the chill rolls has already been made, and it would be quite expensive to alter their positions. However, one way in which most chill roll installations can be made to function more efficiently, with a minimum of cost, is to provide properly installed plumbing.

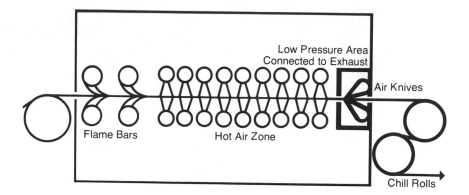

Cross section of gas flame and hot air dryer and chill roll arrangement on web offset press.

With properly installed plumbing, the faster the chill water flows through the individual chill rolls, the more uniform the web temperature will be from side to side. The average temperature of the web will also be slightly lower. Two formulas were used for calculating the effect of chill water flow on web temperature.

Formulas used for calculating the effect of chill water flow.

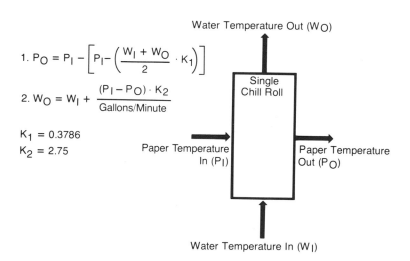

$$1.\ P_O = P_I - \left[P_I - \left(\frac{W_I + W_O}{2} \cdot K_1 \right) \right]$$

$$2.\ W_O = W_I + \frac{(P_I - P_O) \cdot K_2}{\text{Gallons/Minute}}$$

$K_1 = 0.3786$
$K_2 = 2.75$

Three different plumbing methods for chill systems were analyzed by GATF. Each of the systems contained four chill rolls. The manner in which the plumbing is connected to the chill rolls and the order in which the web makes contact with the chill rolls is indicated in the illustration.

Three different plumbing arrangements for chill systems.

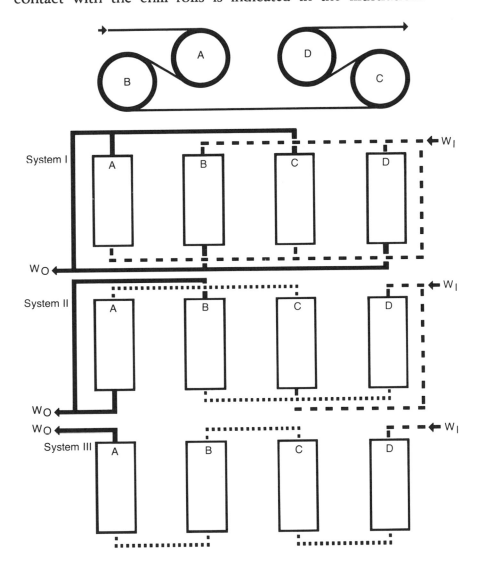

With a 60-gallon-per-minute (227-liter-per-minute) chill water flow rate, the flow rate through each individual chill roll will be 15 gallons per minute (gpm) for System I, 30 gpm for System II, and 60 gpm for System III. The same constants — 1200-feet-per-minute (366-meter-per-minute) press speed, 50°F (10°C) water supply temperature, 38-inch (965-millimeter) web width, and 60-pound (89-grams-per-square meter) book paper — are used for calculating the temperatures for all three systems; the only difference is the flow rate through the chill rolls of the different systems.

Web and water temperature data for the three chill systems diagramed.

Average Web Temperatures through Chill System

	System I °F	System II °F	System III °F
Out of the dryer	310.0	310.0	310.0
After the first chill roll	214.9	214.6	214.5
After the second chill roll	154.5	154.2	153.9
After the third chill roll	116.3	115.4	115.3
After the last chill roll	92.0	91.1	90.8

Water Temperature Rise through Chill Rolls

Chill Rolls	System I °F	System II °F	System III °F
A	17.4	8.7	4.3
B	11.1	5.6	2.8
C	7.0	3.6	1.8
D	4.4	2.2	1.1
Average	10.0	5.0	2.5

Side-to-Side Web Temperature after Chilling

System I	System II	System III
89.8-94.4°F	90.0-92.2°F	90.3-91.4°F

From the data contained in the figure, it can be seen that there is an advantage in increasing the flow of the chill water through the individual chill rolls. A slightly lower average web temperature will result, but the main advantage is that the temperature variations from side to side will be minimized. All chill systems benefit from increased chill water flow, regardless of the number of chill rolls involved.

The drying of heatset inks removes a considerable amount of moisture from the web. The amount of moisture remaining is dependent upon several variables: the ink, amount of ink coverage, the paper, and the type and design of the dryer. In any case, the product delivered has less moisture content than is desirable. For this reason, remoisturizing should be a normal part of any heatset printing operation. Benefits of remoisturizing include printed products that will not change size after trimming due to moisture pickup, fewer problems with static on the press, and signatures or sheets that will be much easier to handle in subsequent bindery operations.

There are several quite adequate remoisturizing systems on the market. These systems range from direct sprays to brush sprays to several different types of roller applicators. Some systems are promoted as "silicone applicators." These are sold as single units that are used on the underside of the web and used only when marking is a problem. Both sides of the web should be remoisturized whenever heat is used as the drying medium.

This section on "Dryer and Chill Stand Troubles" is intended to give the web offset pressman a ready reference that will help him: (1) avoid dryer and chill stand problems; (2) diagnose a problem quickly and correctly when it arises; (3) apply the proper remedy. Some of the remedies may not be possible under existing operating conditions — the press may not have the equipment or devices mentioned in the suggested remedy; it may not be possible to change the paper at the time; doctoring heatset inks should be avoided. For a chronic dryer and chill stand trouble that can only be overcome with equipment or devices not on the press, the suggested remedy may serve as a guide to management in its investigations of new equipment. Where a remedy suggests changing paper or paper specifications, it is assumed that the paper supplier will be called in as soon as the trouble is identified as a paper problem; and correspondingly, the ink supplier when ink is concerned. For details on handling paper and paper complaints, see the "Paper Troubles" section.

The following are the troubles that occur most commonly in the dryer and chill stand sections of blanket-to-blanket web offset presses:

Trouble: **Ink fails to dry, marks** on chill rolls, and smears in delivery.

Cause A: Web temperature reached in the dryer is not high enough to drive off sufficient ink solvents.

Remedy 1:
Adjust the flame bars so that the flame tips impinge properly on the web.

Remedy 2:
Raise the temperature of the air circulating in the dryer.

Remedy 3:
Reduce the press speed.

Remedy 4:
Increase the air velocity in the dryer to cut through and remove the thin air and vapor layer that clings to the moving web.

Remedy 5:
Change to a faster drying ink containing solvents that have a lower boiling point or resins that have better solvent release. A limit is reached when the inks dry and "tack up"

in the printing units. Tackiness, however, can be minimized by water-cooling the vibrating ink drums. When changing inks, consult the inkmaker.

Cause B: Dryer is not long enough or is not properly engineered for the speed of the press or the type of work.

Remedy:
Reduce the press speed or consider purchasing a properly engineered dryer.

Cause C: Not enough chill capacity to reduce web temperature to 90°F (32°C).

Remedy 1:
Reduce the temperature of the cooling water or increase its circulation.

Remedy 2:
Reduce the press speed and the dryer temperature.

Remedy 3:
Add additional chill rolls.

Cause D: Running a heavyweight paper or a heavy ink lay or both.

Remedy 1:
Adjust the flame bars so that the flame tips impinge properly on the web.

Remedy 2:
Raise the temperature of the air circulating in the dryer.

Remedy 3:
Reduce the press speed.

Remedy 4:
Increase the air velocity in the dryer to cut through and remove the thin air and vapor layer that clings to the moving web.

Remedy 5:
Change to a faster drying ink containing solvents that have a lower boiling point or resins that have better solvent release. A limit is reached when the inks dry and "tack up" in the printing units. Tackiness, however, can be minimized by water-cooling the vibrating ink drums. When changing inks, consult the inkmaker.

Cause E: The temperature of the web leaving the dryer is not uniform from side to side. This can be checked by running the web through the dryer without printing on the web. Measurements can be made with a hand-held thermocouple or infrared pyrometer.

Remedy 1:
Clean the flame bars and make sure that the flame impingement is uniform across the web.

Remedy 2:
Clean the air knives or scavengers to assure an even flow of hot air across the web.

Remedy 3:
Have maintenance performed on the dryer by qualified personnel.

Trouble: **Ink dries unevenly.**

Cause: Plate dampening is uneven or erratic.

Remedy 1:
Keep dampener covers clean and free from accumulated ink.

Remedy 2:
Prevent drafts. Several possible sources of drafts are: windows, doors, air-conditioning vents, forced-air humidifiers, and heaters.

Trouble: **Ink sets off** in the folder or delivery although it appears to be dry on leaving chill rolls.

Cause: The ink has surface-dried only in the dryer and is wet underneath. After chilling, the ink's solvent works toward and softens the surface, causing setoff. This is most likely to occur with heavy lays of ink on hard, nonabsorbent papers.

Remedy:
Reduce speed of the press. If the slower web overheats, reduce the dryer temperature. Maximum web temperature should not exceed 375°F (190°C).

Trouble: **Ink is still tacky** after it leaves the chill rolls, causing setoff or sticking.

Cause: Chill rollers are not cooling the printed web enough to harden and set the resin ink binder. The web is not cool to the touch; web temperature is not down to 90°F (32°C) after chilling.

Remedy 1:
Increase the flow rate of the cooling water, provided it is cold enough to do the job. If not, install an evaporative cooler or refrigerating unit to supply colder water.

Remedy 2:
Check the water temperature at outlets of the rollers. If the water is cold enough but the web temperature is too high, the chill rolls may be fouled with a mineral deposit from the water. Remove this by flushing out the rolls. The fouling can be prevented from forming by the use of a system in which the water is recirculated.

Remedy 3:
If the water is cold enough, but the web temperature is too high, the chill rolls may not have sufficient area. If this is the case, increase the number of chill rolls.

Remedy 4:
If the ink is set properly near one edge of the web but remains tacky near the other edge, there must be a temperature gradient across the chill rolls. In this case,

change the plumbing to the chill rolls to give a more efficient chill system. See the introduction to this section for a discussion of plumbing methods.

Remedy 5:
Reduce the press speed and the dryer temperature.

Paper scorches or discolors in the dryer.

Cause: Dryer temperature is too high for the web speed.

Remedy 1:
Lower the temperature in the dryer.

Remedy 2:
Increase the web speed if the chilling capacity is sufficient.

Trouble: **Ink changes in hue** or loses brightness on passing through dryer.

Cause A: Heat resistance of ink pigments is too low for the dryer temperature. Reds are the most susceptible to change.

Remedy 1:
Reduce dryer temperature, and reduce press speed if necessary.

Remedy 2:
Get inks that contain more heat-resistant pigments. Consult the inkmaker.

Cause B: Excessive heat in the dryer results in too much penetration of the ink vehicle resin and loss of gloss. Ink is overdried.

Remedy 1:
Reduce dryer temperature.

Remedy 2:
Increase the press speed if the chilling capacity is sufficient.

Cause C: Paper is too absorbent for the ink. The ink may penetrate too much, even before entering dryer.

Remedy 1:
Have the ink reformulated for less penetration.

Remedy 2:
Change to a paper that is less absorbent.

Trouble: **Ink gloss is reduced or lost in dryer.**

Cause: Excessive ink-vehicle penetration into web.

Remedy 1:
Reduce the heat in the dryer to reduce the web temperature.

Remedy 2:
Increase press speed to reduce the web temperature if the chilling capacity is sufficient.

Remedy 3:
Obtain inks that have better holdout.

Trouble: **Coated paper blisters** during passage through the dryer. Such blistering of paper in the dryer should not be confused with delamination that can occur in the press printing units.

Blisters formed in coated paper because of too rapid heating of the printed web in the dryer, too much moisture in the paper, or too heavy a lay of ink.
Courtesy of Consolidated Papers, Inc.

Blisters occurring in the dryer are almost round, have sharp edges, and are visible on both sides of the sheet. They can occur anywhere on the sheet, although they are most likely to be found in areas of solids, especially if these are backed up with solids. Blisters never occur with uncoated papers.

Delamination due to ink tack is visible as elongated blisters with indefinite edges and is usually only on one side of the sheet. Delamination occurs only where solids or heavy halftones are backed up with similar printed areas. It never occurs in unprinted areas. It can occur with smooth uncoated as well as coated stocks, and even when no heat dryer is used. See "Printing Unit Troubles: Paper is Delaminated."

Cause A: The paper has too high a moisture content. At dryer temperature, the excess moisture changes to high-pressure water vapor, which can rupture the interior of the paper if the water vapor cannot escape fast enough.

Remedy 1:
Specify that paper should have a lower moisture content.

Remedy 2:
Install a preheater in the press infeed. This will reduce and even out the paper's moisture content.

Remedy 3:
In a multistage dryer, turn down the line burners or reduce their impingement on the web. Raise the temperature of the circulating air, if necessary, to produce drying. Blisters are caused by the rapid vaporization of moisture when the web is heated too fast or to too high a temperature.

Remedy 4:
Reduce the press speed and the dryer temperature. This slows the moisture vaporization and thereby permits the water vapor to escape through the pores of the coating without rupture.

Remedy 5:
Increase the speed of the press without changing the dryer conditions. This action reduces the maximum web temperature.

Remedy 6:
Obtain paper which has a more porous coating. In general, letterpress coatings are more porous and resist blistering better than do litho coatings. Double-coated or blade-coated litho papers are the most susceptible to blistering.

Cause B:
Printing of heavyweight coated stock. At 4% moisture content, an 80-lb. book paper contains twice as much moisture per square inch as a 40-lb. book paper does, and twice as much moisture must escape at drying temperature.

Remedy:
Run heavy stock at reduced web speeds and low dryer temperatures. Heavy webs require longer dryers.

Cause C:
Printing solids with heavy ink coverage, especially when back-to-back. Ink fills the pores of the coating and slows down the escape of water vapor. Blistering can occur in heavy ink solids only, while none occurs in halftone or blank areas.

Remedy 1:
Change to a more pigmented ink and print less of it to minimize blocking of the coating pores. This practice may not produce the desired gloss but will minimize blocking of the coating pores.

Remedy 2:
Try the remedies listed under "Coated Paper Blisters, Cause A."

Trouble:
Web corrugates in dryer. Sometimes this causes wrinkles to form as the web passes over the chill rolls. Corrugation can also cause streaks in the printing if the depressions are deep enough to contact parts of the dryer.

Corrugations are wrinkles that form in the press direction. The longer the span of unsupported web in the dryer, the higher the web tension, and the lighter the web weight, the greater is the tendency of the paper to corrugate.

Cause: The span of the unsupported web is too long, the web tension is too high, or the web is too light in weight; or any combination of the three.

Remedy 1:
Reduce the tension in the dryer.

Remedy 2:
Change to a heavier weight of paper.

Remedy 3:
Install grater rollers or air bars to minimize the length of unsupported web in the dryer.

11 Delivery Troubles

Introduction Web offset is extremely versatile with regard to delivery. Most presses are equipped with a folder, of which there are several kinds. Folders are designed for specific types of jobs, but vary in flexibility as to the page size they can handle and the number of folds they can produce. Some presses have auxiliary equipment for such operations as imprinting, numbering, punching, perforating, interleaving, gluing, and bundling. Each of these operations involves special problems that require knowledge and experience to solve. This section will be confined to a discussion of troubles that stem from paper and ink and from the printing, drying, and chilling operations.

Some presses are equipped with sheeters, usually in addition to a folder. In such cases, remoisturizing the web is usually necessary to remove static and enable proper delivery and jogging of the sheets. Incidentally, such equipment may help to prevent cracking at the folds. This is accomplished by means of moisture applicators. There are several successful systems available all of which return an appreciable amount of moisture to the web. Because of the amount of moisture these systems reapply to the web, GATF recommends that they be used on both sides of the web whenever heatset ink drying is a part of the printing operation. Remoisturized signatures will prove less troublesome in bindery operations and will be less likely to change size after binding because of subsequent moisture absorption. The remoisturizer should be located after the chill rolls.

This section on "Delivery Troubles" is intended to give the web offset pressman a ready reference that will help him: (1) avoid delivery problems; (2) quickly and correctly diagnose a problem when it arises; (3) apply the proper remedy. Some of the remedies may not be possible under existing operating conditions — the press may not have the equipment or devices mentioned in the suggested remedy; it may not be possible to change the paper at the time; doctoring heatset inks should be avoided. For a chronic delivery trouble that can only be overcome with equipment or devices which are not available, the suggested remedy may serve as a guide to management in its investigations of new equipment. Where a remedy suggests changing paper or paper specifications, it is assumed that the paper supplier will be called in as soon as the trouble is identified as a paper problem; and correspondingly, the ink supplier when ink is concerned. For details on handling paper and paper complaints, see the introduction to the "Paper Troubles" section.

The principal troubles in folding and delivery are as follows:

Trouble: **Web sags** going into the folder, causing variable cutoff misregister.

Cause A: Overpacked blankets in the printing unit.

Remedy 1:
If the blanket packing is higher than normal, reduce it by removing 0.001" (0.025 mm) or more of the packing from each blanket and readjusting the blanket-to-blanket pressure if necessary.

Remedy 2:
Check the diameter of the driven rollers feeding the folder. If web sags are a chronic problem, these rollers may be undersized.

Cause B: Insufficient web tension: the speed of the chill rolls is too high or the folder speed is too low.

Remedy:
Increase the speed of the folder slightly or decrease the speed of the chill rolls until the web is under normal tension.

Trouble: **Gusset wrinkles.**

Cause: Paper is too stiff or heavy to be folded smoothly into a closed-head signature. The problem is created when the cross fold is made. At this time, because of the mechanics of the fold, the inside sheets of the signature want to move away from the backbone but are prevented from moving freely because they are tied, through the closed head, to the outside sheets. If enough stress is created, a gusset wrinkle will form.

Remedy:
Perforate along the head to allow the inside and outside sheets to move relative to each other. The more paper removed by the perforation, the less chance there is for a gusset wrinkle to occur.

Trouble: **Wrinkling on former.**

Cause: The former board is not lined up perfectly with the direction of web travel.

Remedy 1:
Change the angle of the former board slightly.

Remedy 2:
Perforate the center of the web before it comes down over the former board.

Trouble: **Cutoff misregister.**

Cause: Poor control of web tension somewhere in the press from the infeed to the folder or sheeter cutoff.

Remedy 1:
Check the roll of paper on the infeed. If it is tapered or shows flats or welts, replace it with a good roll.

Remedy 2:
Equip the press with a constant-tension infeed.

Remedy 3:
Check for shrinkage in the dryer. This condition could be to blame if the folder overpulls the paper or if the web pulls out of the jaws. Reduce the folder speed or increase the chill roll speed.

Remedy 4:
Check electronic cutoff control and adjust for proper operation.

Trouble: **Side lay varies.**

Cause A: Side lay of the printing is varying because of weaving of the web at the infeed. This could be caused by welts, corrugations, or soft spots in the paper roll.

Remedy:
Check the paper roll for defects and replace roll if necessary.

Cause B: Too much air used on angle bars of ribbon folder. This could cause the webs to stray sideways and be out of register with each other.

Remedy 1:
Reduce the air pressure on the angle bars until side-slippage stops.

Remedy 2:
Increase tension in the angle bar section.

Trouble: **Poor folding.**

Cause A: The paper is too dry, having been dehydrated excessively while in the dryer. This dryness causes roughness and cracking at the fold.

Remedy 1:
Use remoisturizing equipment to put moisture back into the paper. Refer to the introduction of this section.

Remedy 2:
Reduce the dryer temperature until it is just high enough to dry the ink.

Cause B: The paper is too bulky to fold well and produces signatures that are too bulky. Assuming that the paper is not too dry, the following may help:

Remedy 1:
Slit the web ahead of the former fold if possible.

Remedy 2:
Heavily perforate the web ahead of the former fold.

Trouble: **Smudging and scuffing** in folder.

Cause A: Ink has not dried hard enough. This trouble may occur if the dryer has not had enough time to heat up.

Remedy 1:
Preheat the dryer before the start-up.

Remedy 2:
Raise the dryer temperature or increase the hot air circulation, or both.

Remedy 3:
Reduce the dryer temperature and the press speed if the ink is surface-dried but is wet underneath.

Cause B: The web has not been properly chilled and the resinous ink binder is still soft. The web temperature should not be higher than about 90°F (32°C) on leaving the chill rolls; this will be cool to the touch.

Remedy 1:
Reduce the temperature of the chill rolls. If cooling water temperature is too high, use refrigeration.

Remedy 2:
Be sure that the chill rolls have an efficient plumbing system. (See introduction to "Dryer and Chill Stand Troubles.") If the chill rolls have efficient plumbing, then increase the flow rate of the chill water.

Remedy 3:
Reduce the press speed and the dryer temperature.

Cause C: As the web leaves the dryer, solvent vapors cling to it, condense on chilling, and soften the dried ink.

Remedy:
Add an effective scavenging device to remove the solvent vapors. Such a device usually consists of a pair of air knives located just inside the point of exit from the dryer.

Cross section of a heat dryer with an air knife scavenger at web exit.

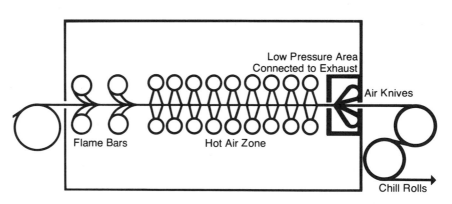

Cause D: Too much friction at the former nose.

Remedy 1:
Reduce the folder speed slightly or increase the speed of the chill rolls to reduce web tension.

Remedy 2:
Apply a coating on the former nose to decrease the friction. A coating of Teflon tape helps, but it must be renewed frequently. A special thick tape is made for this purpose.

Cause E: Angle bars on the ribbon folders are marking the web. Marking may be due to the ink's being soft (Causes A, B, and C) or possibly to an angle bar that is not set at the correct angle.

Remedy 1:
Increase the air on the angle bars.

Remedy 2:
If an angle bar is at an incorrect angle, reset it.

Trouble: **Static and curl** cause excessive spoilage on the sheeter.

Cause A: The paper is charged with static electricity and fails to deliver and jog properly.

Remedy 1:
Check the dryer temperature and adjust if too high. The heat may be removing too much moisture from the paper.

Remedy 2:
Check the temperature of the web leaving the chill rollers. If higher than about 90°F (32°C), increase the flow rate or refrigerate the cooling water.

Remedy 3:
Remoisturize the paper. Remoisturizing is the most effective method of combatting static, but the web must be cool. (Refer to the introduction to this section.)

Remedy 4:
Install antistatic tapes in the sheeter.

Cause B: Paper curl prevents proper delivery and jogging. Curl is generally due to excessive drying of the paper.

Remedy 1:
Check the dryer temperature and adjust if too high.

Remedy 2:
Remoisturize the paper. (Refer to the introduction to this section.)

12 Print Quality Troubles

Introduction   In the early stages of web offset's development, print quality was poor in comparison to that of sheetfed offset. As a result of various improvements and the experience gained over the years in practical production, web offset has become established as a quality printing method. Web offset printing is now capable of quality printing competitive with sheetfed offset, letterpress, and gravure. But such quality is not always attained and often involves excessive waste. There are still many problems to be solved. Research and development work is being carried on by machinery manufacturers, suppliers, and by GATF; and the number and the severity of problems are being reduced.

One of the problems towards the attainment of uniformly high print quality is the shortage of highly skilled operators. Web offset has experienced rapid expansion, and time is required to train and develop men capable of producing the high quality desired. This book is intended to help solve this problem by providing dependable information on the causes and remedies for the troubles most commonly encountered in pressrooms.

Web offset already has proved its ability to produce high-quality printing. Now the target of most research and development is adequate quality controls to enable consistent attainment of high quality. Press controls are being improved, and electronic controls for color and register are being introduced. These controls are a step in the right direction; they should relieve operators from making continuous inspection and from making frequent manual press adjustments, and should allow more time for preparation, maintenance, and housekeeping. However, the controls will need highly skilled operators to keep them working properly and will never replace human knowledge and experience. Properly handled, the controls will definitely improve quality and production, and reduce waste.

A number of quality control devices have been designed for use with offset presses. However, a number of these do not lend themselves to use in web offset printing because of their size. Three quality control devices that can usually be used in web offset printing — and their uses — are as follows:

1. The GATF "Star Target," a 0.375-inch (9.6-millimeter) target that gives information on resolution and dot spread and also shows and discriminates between slurring and doubling.

2. The GATF "Quality Control (QC) Strip," a strip 0.125 inch (3.2 millimeters) wide that is designed to show changes in sharpness, density, and ink-water balance in color images.

3. The GATF "Compact Color Test Strip," a strip 0.25 inch (6.4 millimeters) wide that includes Star Targets and the various color patches needed to provide complete information on printed color images.

Additional information concerning these quality control devices is contained in GATF Research Progress Reports available from Graphic Arts Technical Foundation, 4615 Forbes Ave., Pittsburgh, Pa. 15213.

Prepress problems create a great deal of trouble in the pressroom. These problems concern both the quality and the placement of the image on the plate. It is possible — and it should be the goal of every prepress department — to furnish plates to the pressroom which never have to be cocked on the press nor require an extensive amount of fountain key adjustment to achieve the desired results. To obtain the best possible image quality requires the cooperation of people outside the printing plant; this cooperation has proven to be an elusive goal so far. The control of image placement, however, is within the ability of the average printing plant; it should be the goal of every printer to completely eliminate any press adjustments to achieve proper register. There are several register systems available today that are capable of making this goal possible if used with an adequate bending jig. The requirements for a bending jig are listed in the GATF publication *Web Offset Press Operating*.

This section on "Print Quality Troubles" is intended to give the web offset pressman a ready reference to help him: (1) avoid print quality problems; (2) diagnose a problem quickly and correctly when it arises; (3) apply the proper remedy. Some of the remedies may not be possible under existing operating conditions — the press may not have the equipment or devices mentioned in the suggested remedy; it may not be possible to change the paper at the time; doctoring heatset inks should be avoided. For a chronic print quality trouble that can only be overcome with equipment or devices not available on the press, the suggested remedy may serve as a guide to management in its investigations of new equipment. Where a remedy suggests changing paper or paper specifications, it is assumed that the paper supplier will be called in as soon as the trouble is identified as a paper problem; and correspondingly, the ink supplier when ink is concerned. For details on handling paper and paper complaints, see the "Paper Troubles" section.

In this section we are listing the main troubles that affect print quality and their causes and known remedies. If any of these have been covered in previous sections, proper references will be made.

Trouble: **Misregister in the running direction.** Web offset presses have adjustments, either manual or mechanical, for bringing the work into proper position on the web, for bringing the colors into register, and for synchronizing the cutoff with the printed work. Trouble arises only when some condition prevents consistently good register, once the proper adjustments have been made.

Cause A: One or more plates are cocked or are not properly registered on their cylinders.

Remedy:
Handle plates more carefully on the bending jig. The recommended practice is for **one** experienced operator to do all bending of plates. At least two men should mount a

23x35" (584x885-mm) plate, and three men are needed to mount a 35x50" (885x1,270-mm) plate.

Cause B: One or more plates are printing longer or shorter than the others.

Remedy:
Transfer the packing from blanket to plate to shorten the print; or from plate to blanket to lengthen the print. Maintain good tension on the web.

Cause C: Uneven blanket packing. If one of the printing units is not pulling the web fast enough, web tension between it and the following unit will build up until the web snaps back, causing misregister.

Remedy:
Adjust blanket packing until the draws between the units are equal.

Cause D: Web tension is too low; the higher the tension, the better the register.

Remedy:
Increase the web tension in the infeed section of the press. If the press is not equipped with a constant-tension infeed it should be added.

Cause E: Web tension changes during run, probably because infeed tension changes.

Remedy:
Equip the press with a constant-tension infeed.

Cause F: Ink tack is too high. This tackiness may cause excessive variations in the wrap of the web on blankets in areas of solids, momentarily increasing tension on parts of the web. The local stretch of these parts can affect running register.

Remedy 1:
Reduce the tack of the inks that are printing the troublesome solids.

Remedy 2:
Increase the web tension.

Remedy 3:
Reduce the press speed.

NOTE: Ink tack can be changed temporarily by press stops and starts. Such change can be minimized by water-cooling the ink drums.

Cause G: Piling of paper coating on blanket, changing the blanket's diameter.

Remedy 1:
Wash up blanket frequently.

Remedy 2:
Change to a more moisture-resistant paper.

Cause H: Speed of press has been changed without a correction in the web tension.

Remedy 1:
Equip the press with a constant-tension infeed.

Remedy 2:
Adjust the web tension until register is obtained.

Remedy 3:
Increase the distance traveled by the web between the infeed and the first printing unit.

Cause I: A roll of paper out of round, or a roll containing flats.

Remedy 1:
Equip the press with a constant-tension infeed.

Remedy 2:
Increase the distance traveled by the web between the infeed and the first printing unit.

Remedy 3:
Change to a good roll.

Trouble: **Side-to-side misregister** is more likely to occur with wide webs. Some pressmen feel that webs wider than 30-35 inches (760-890 millimeters) are not satisfactory for high-quality work.

Cause A: Nonuniform moisture content across the web causes corrugation of roll and side-to-side misregister.

Remedy 1:
Increase the distance traveled by the web between the infeed and the first printing unit. The longer the distance and the higher the web tension, the more uniform the web will be.

Remedy 2:
Use a preheater on the infeed to dry the paper some, to even out moisture content, and to flatten the web.

Remedy 3:
Equip the press with a Mount Hope or similar curved roller to spread and flatten the web. See "Paper Troubles: Roll is Corrugated."

Cause B: Welts caused by unwrapping rolls in a high-humidity area and allowing them to stand for some time. Such welts are rarely more than 0.25 inch (6.4 millimeters) deep. This small amount of corrugation will cause some side-to-side misregister just after splicing.

Remedy 1:
Slab of the outer 0.25 inch (6.4 millimeters) of paper.

Remedy 2:
Do not unwrap rolls until just before going to press. See "Paper Troubles" section.

Cause C: Paper varies in caliper across the web.

Remedy:
Increase the distance traveled by the web between the infeed and the first printing unit. The longer the distance and the higher the web tension, the more uniform the web will be.

Cause D: Web has slack edges due to moisture pickup while in the roll.

Remedy 1:
Prevention. Keep rolls protected from atmospheric changes until they are mounted on the infeed stand. See Section 8, "Paper Troubles."

Remedy 2:
Increase the distance traveled by the web between the infeed and the first printing unit. The longer the distance and the higher the web tension, the more uniform the web will be.

Remedy 3:
Increase the web tension. Stretching the web tends to tighten slack edges.

Remedy 4:
Equip the press with a Mount Hope or similar curved roller on the infeed to spread and flatten the web. See "Paper Troubles: Roll Is Corrugated."

Remedy 5:
Adjust the eccentric-mounted infeed roller to balance edge tension.

Cause E: Ink tack is too high and causes excessive wrap of the web on blankets in areas of solids, momentarily increasing tension on parts of the web. The local stretch of these parts can affect running register, side-to-side register, and cutoff register.

Remedy 1:
Reduce the tack of the inks printing the troublesome solids.

Remedy 2:
Increase the web tension.

Remedy 3:
Reduce the press speed.

NOTE: Ink tack can be changed temporarily by press stops and starts. Such change can be minimized by water-cooling the ink drums.

Trouble: **First-down color is wider across the web than later colors.**

This condition, usually called fan-out, is the result of a natural tendency of a web, which is under relatively high tension as it comes off the infeed roll, to shorten and become wider as it is subjected to the lower tensions encountered within the press. Fan-out and its control is discussed in detail in the GATF publication *Web Offset Press Operating*. The primary method of controlling fan-out is to use bustle wheels on the press and, in some cases, by progressively stepping out the images on the plates. The problem becomes more severe as the web goes through the press because it takes time for the paper to adjust to the lower tension condition of the press. The longer the web is allowed to run at press tension before it enters the first printing unit, the better is the result. This improvement is one of the advantages gained by the use of a festoon-type splicer. Generally, increasing the length of the web lead in the infeed section of the press will reduce the amount of fan-out between printed images.

Bustle wheel used under the web to overcome fan-out and resulting misregister.

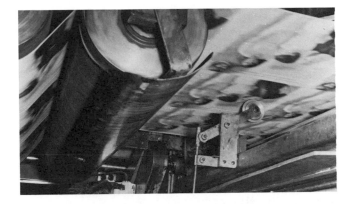

Cause A: Moisture applied by the printing units. Although fan-out is not affected by the amount of moisture in the paper, it is very sensitive to additional moisture added by the printing units.

Remedy:
Run with a minimum of dampening solution.

Cause B: Web tension is less between printing units than at the infeed. The initial stretch of the web, therefore, decreases in the printing section and allows the web width to increase after the first color is down, making the succeeding colors print narrower.

Remedy 1:
Decrease web tension at the infeed.

Remedy 2:
Increase the web tension in the printing section of the press.

Cause C: Tension on the paper, once it leaves the roll and travels through the press, is much less than the tension under which the roll was wound at the mill. The high mill-winding tension (essential to produce well-running rolls) stretches the paper in the grain direction and shrinks it in the across-the-grain direction. Relieving the tension (which occurs after the paper leaves the roll) permits the paper to relax and, therefore, become wider in the across-the-grain direction as the paper travels through the press.

Remedy 1:
Increase tension in the press to the highest practical limit conducive to good production.

Remedy 2:
Pass the paper over as many rollers as possible between the unwind stand and the first unit to allow as much time as possible for the paper to relax.

Trouble: **Printing lacks sharpness**, even with good plates.

Cause A: Inks are too soft for the press speed. Normally, the stiffer the ink, the sharper the plate will print, especially the halftones.

Remedy 1:
Increase press speed. Many pressmen report that best print quality is achieved at high speeds.

Remedy 2:
Consult the inkmaker about getting tackier inks, if press is running at maximum speed. Consider adding gellants to the ink.

Cause B: Too much dampening or nonuniform dampening. Molleton dampeners may be worn or dirty.

Remedy 1:
Cut down dampening to a minimum.

Remedy 2:
Clean or replace faulty dampeners.

Remedy 3:
Try using paper dampener covers. (Special rollers are required for these covers.)

Cause C:　Slurring or doubling of halftone dots.

　Remedy:
　See "Printing Unit Troubles: Slurring" and "Printing Unit Troubles: Doubling."

Cause D:　Line and halftone work on plate not sharp enough to compensate for normal press gain.

　Remedy:
　Obtain cooperation of photo and plate departments in providing suitable plates to compensate for dot gain on the press.

Trouble:　**Solids lack good ink coverage.**

Cause A:　Printing is snowflaky as a result of excessive dampening water being taken up by the ink. When the ink film is split, water droplets are exposed. These droplets prevent uniform ink transfer to the paper.

　Remedy:
　Reduce the water feed. If the ink on the rollers appears to be waterlogged (the ink length is greatly shortened by the moisture), change to an ink that is resistant to waterlogging.

Cause B:　Roughness of some uncoated papers.

　Remedy 1:
　Increase the blanket-to-blanket pressure.

　Remedy 2:
　Soften the inks somewhat to improve their coverage.

　Remedy 3:
　Change to compressible blankets.

Trouble: **Solids are mottled.**

Cause: There is heavy paper linting on the press. It is necessary to wash blankets frequently. Blankets do not appear to be excessively tacky.

Remedy 1:
Run less water to prevent softening of paper.

Remedy 2:
Increase blanket packing 0.002" (0.05 mm). The additional pressure will help to scrub the collected material off the blankets.

Trouble: **Printing lacks gloss or finish.** One advantage of web offset is its ability to produce glossy printing without the use of antisetoff sprays. Quick evaporation of the solvent reduces absorption of ink vehicle by the paper, giving good ink holdout, which is one factor in producing gloss. Other factors affecting this are paper smoothness and paper gloss. These characteristics are the reason that the bulk of color work is done on coated papers. High gloss is desirable because it enhances the brilliance and intensity of colors. Failure to obtain gloss may be due to one or more of the following causes:

Cause A: The ink vehicle is too fluid or the paper is too absorbent, or both.

Remedy 1:
Have inkmaker formulate a suitable ink for the conditions.

Remedy 2:
Change to a less absorbent paper or a paper with a coating designed to give better ink holdout.

Cause B: Preheating of the web at the infeed. The hot paper warms the press and reduces the viscosity of the ink vehicles, increasing ink penetrating power.

Remedy:
Reduce the temperature of the preheater, omit the preheater entirely, or install chill rollers between the preheater and the first printing unit.

Cause C: Too high a temperature in the dryer makes the resin binder too fluid and penetrating, causing reduced gloss. The result is sometimes called "fried ink."

Remedy:
Reduce the dryer temperature or increase the speed of the press. Have the ink reformulated with a more volatile solvent to enable the dryer temperature to be reduced.

Cause D: Running with too much dampening solution. Excessive moisture in the ink prevents the smooth ink lay necessary for high gloss.

Remedy:
Reduce the dampening water to a minimum.

Cause E: The ink is too highly pigmented. This produces a situation where insufficient binder remains on the paper to completely cover all of the pigment particles and where some of the pigment particles poke through the surface, destroying gloss.

Remedy:
Consult with the ink maker.

Trouble: **Ghost images** appear in solids or halftones.

Cause A: A narrow solid ahead of or behind a wider solid is robbing the form rollers of the ink needed to print full strength color in the corresponding area of the wider solid. The same result is noticeable in darker halftones.

Remedy 1:
Whenever possible, make layouts with solids and halftones well distributed.

Remedy 2:
Run a minimum of dampening water.

Remedy 3:
Avoid running colors spare to product tints. Make the color weaker and run more of it.

Remedy 4:
If possible, use opaque inks rather than transparent inks.

Remedy 5:
Cut down on the movement of the vibrating drums to enable more ink to be confined to narrow areas of high demand. In some cases ghosting will be reduced.

Cause B: The blanket is embossed as a result of ink-vehicle absorption during printing of the previous job.

Remedy:
Install a new blanket.

NOTE: Clean an embossed blanket thoroughly with blanket wash and hang it in a dark area to rest. Resting will allow absorbed oil to diffuse through the rubber and may reduce the embossing.

Trouble: **Fiber-puffing** appears as an overall roughness, usually in the printing areas. This occurs only on paper made from groundwood pulp.

Cause: The water contained in small clumps of fibers is being changed to water vapor too rapidly and is causing the clumps to burst. This gives the paper a rough, sandpaper-like finish.

Remedy 1:
Run press slower to reduce thermal shock in dryer.

Remedy 2:
Use paper which does not contain groundwood pulp.

Other quality defects in web offset printing, and their causes and remedies, are discussed in previous sections as follows:

Section 11   **Delivery Troubles**
Gusset Wrinkles Develop
Cutoff Misregister
Side Lay Varies
Poor Folding
Smudging and Scuffing

Index